CLOTH DOLL ARTISTRY

DESIGN AND COSTUMING TECHNIQUES FOR FLAT AND FULLY SCULPTED FIGURES

BEVERLY MASSACHUSETTS

QUARRY BOOKS

BARBARA WILLIS

First published in the United States of America by
Quarry Books, a member of
Quayside Publishing Group
100 Cummings Center
Suite 406-L
Beverly, Massachusetts 01915-6101
Telephone: (978) 282-9590
Fax: (978) 283-2742
www.quarrybooks.com

Library of Congress Cataloging-in-Publication Data
Willis, Barbara (Barbara E.)
  Cloth doll artistry : design and costuming techniques for flat and fully sculpted figures /
Barbara Willis.
      p. cm.
ISBN-13: 978-1-59253-513-2
ISBN-10: 1-59253-513-5
1. Dollmaking. 2. Doll clothes--Patterns. 3. Cloth dolls. I. Title.
TT175.W548 2009
745.592'21--dc22

                                                                        2008052262
                                                                        CIP

ISBN-13: 978-1-59253-513-2
ISBN-10: 1-59253-513-5

10 9 8 7 6 5 4 3 2

Design: Carol Holtz
Production and Layout: Rachel Fitzgibbon, studio rkf
Photography: Bob Hirsch
Illustrations and Templates: Lisa Li Hertzi

Printed in Singapore

生五上棕黑符
爾要的地方，敬

Contents

Introduction

Cloth doll making is a creative art form that lets us play and explore in a personal way. As the dolls begin to take shape, we engage with them and give our imagination wings. The projects in this book will help you fly with new, expressive, and artistic wings of your own. This book is for anyone who ever wanted to make a cloth doll. There are no prerequisites, no limits—and no stopping once you get going!

In one form or another, dolls have been part of my life as long as I can remember. Fabric is another love of mine, so the two passions are perfectly matched. Creating fabric dolls allows me to explore them together.

My dolls are the outflow of a lifetime love of color, texture, form, and creativity. Each doll is a part of me, a journey we take together. For years I have been collecting vintage trims, ribbons, buttons, and charms, and have been haunting antique shops, garage sales, and the Paris flea market. I adore the search for these special treasures, as each doll demands her own look and style.

All creativity starts with decisions about the basic elements of color, texture, and form, and this is where this book begins. You will learn how to select, gather, sort, and layer fabrics, trims, and beads to set the stage for your doll making. Developing a distinctive color palette defines your doll's statement to the world; this process is sheer play, requiring only your imagination. You will learn to stuff a doll so it is smooth and free of lumps.

Three distinctive styles of cloth doll making are explored in this book. I begin by sharing a vintage image for you to transfer onto fabric to create a flat doll. This is a

playful approach to cloth doll making and a process that can be easily shared with children. Simple beading, rubber-stamping on fabric, and whimsical embellishment are lavished on this flat cloth doll.

The second doll project guides you through cloth doll basics, including the proper terms, tools, and techniques. This beginner-level doll focuses on the fun of creating a three-dimensional cloth doll with a fabulous face and a fanciful costume. You can choose to draw your own facial features with step-by-step instructions or to use a fabric transfer image. I believe anyone can create a lovely face for his or her own doll. Once you have tried the techniques I share in this book, you will be creating fabulous doll faces all on your own.

The third doll project features advanced techniques that allow you to create a full, soft-sculpted face from a knit fabric. It calls for hand-stitching knit fabric to create the mouth, cheeks, and chin, and for finishing the eyes with glass beads. The full facial coloration is done one step at a time to bring the doll to life.

All the pattern pieces are included to create leather shoes, hands with wired fingers, and costumes for these projects. My desire is for this book to be the springboard for your own cloth doll explorations, which you fill with fun and fantasy.

I have asked a few friends to play dolls with me, and their lovely creations in the gallery sections will inspire you. This is a feast for your eyes and your imagination. These dolls make me want to be a better doll maker.

Join me on this artistic journey to make and play with dolls!

—Barbara Willis

 # Getting Started

Choosing Fabrics, Creating a Color Palette, Tools, and Using Basic Techniques

One of the most important decisions you will make as you design your cloth doll is about the cloth itself. Choosing the fabrics for your doll and her costume is the first step. My approach to dolls and their clothing is different than you might expect. The clothes are, in many cases, part of the actual doll construction. I often use silk dupioni for the torso, which serves two purposes: It forms the actual torso while it dresses the upper body.

Invest your time wisely by choosing top-quality fabrics for the doll body. Experience has taught me that closely woven, high-thread-count pima cotton that does not stretch is the best fabric for basic body parts (torso, legs, and arms), and it is essential for the hands and head. Pima cotton is also ideal for stuffing and drawing on, and it resists fraying. Muslin is not a good fabric for a cloth doll body because the weave is unstable and the fabric stretches when you stuff the doll. For soft-sculpted faces, it is essential to use a good knit fabric (page 73).

In general, I use high-thread-count cotton fabrics for the actual body parts, but sometimes I give in to the lure of richer, color-saturated silk dupioni. Even though the silk dupioni slips and frays more than cotton

fabrics, it can be used with careful handling and slightly wider seam allowances (page 25) making them ideal for the doll costumes. Silk dupioni offers a richness and depth of color not often found in other fabrics. It stands up, lies down, gathers, and drapes in beautiful folds, ruffles, and pleats. Do not substitute synthetic fabrics for silk because they don't perform as nicely and you might not be satisfied with the results. If you can't find silk dupioni in your local fabric stores, try the Internet.

Choosing trims is equally important and just as enriching. Collect a good stash of vintage laces and trims, but if your stash is lacking, don't let that hold you back. You can find lovely new laces at local fabric shops, especially in the bridal department. I also love to shop in home décor

departments for tassels, unusual trims, and drapery silks in fabulous colors. Another source for lovely ribbon and trims is scrapbook stores. If you are not a scrapbooker, you may have overlooked this source for a treasure hunt.

Flea markets abound in every state and on every continent, and they are true treasure troves for vintage finds. Of course, you might not love the vintage look, and that is exciting too—because you must love something else!

Individuality is what makes cloth doll making so creative and fun. The dolls truly become a reflection of personalities through style and color choices. Choose the best-quality fabric and trim you can find. You will find a materials and supply list for each doll project in this book so you'll know exactly what you need to collect.

Choosing Fabrics

Color is a personal preference. Color shapes our world and creates a mood or feeling. Color breathes life into our cloth doll art. In this chapter, I share four color boards and four minidresses to demonstrate the many ways of combining fabrics and color. The minidresses should help you interpret the fabrics from the color boards. The dresses are simple statements, but they show how you can create lovely, whimsical, elegant, or sassy doll costumes from a simple stash of fabric. Each board and dress represent a different feeling, mood, and style. They are designed to spark your imagination as you see how you can combine and layer trims, laces, buttons, and charms. Some of the elements shown on the color boards are not scaled proportionately, but this is an exercise in color, texture, layers, and possibility, rather than size. I am not necessarily suggesting that you create an actual color board or minidress before beginning a doll project, but I offer them as a visual way to show the use of color, fabric, and texture for a doll's costume.

Color Wheel

You might want to refer to a color wheel, which clearly shows how colors complement and contrast. Fabric designers create their wonderful arrays of print fabrics by using the magic of the color wheel to select colors that work together. Often, prints and solid fabrics are designed as a cohesive group. You can use these groupings, or creatively mix and match your own selection of fabrics and trims, pulling in varied textures and fibers. Either way, you'll have a doll whose personality is reflected in the colors and patterns of the fabrics and trims you use.

When beginning a new cloth doll project, nothing gives me more pleasure than heaping loads of fabrics, trims, and laces on my worktable. I recommend you do the same: Spend time with your materials, combining and recombining them. Ask yourself: What mood am I in? What fabric catches my eye? What color feels good today?

There are endless choices and possibilities. This is where the fun begins—right in the middle of the fabric stash! For the boards on the following pages, I chose a main fabric and then arranged an assortment of trims around it. I wanted the boards to look fun, so I added a vintage image as the centerpiece. The idea is to choose your main fabric and then select trims, laces, buttons, beads, charms, and all sorts of notions to add texture and make the fabric more interesting.

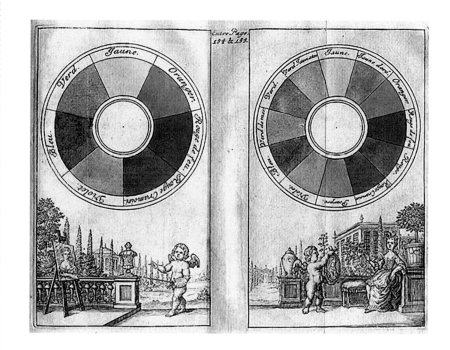

Hand-painted color circles from the 1708 edition of Traitde la Peinture in Mignature, *attributed to Claude Boutet, including the oldest example of the symmetrical 12-hue artists color wheel. Credit: Kuehni (2003).*

Romantic Chic

This romantic color board features a background cotton fabric with a lovely paisley print filled with soft colors that yield an eclectic palette. The paisley would make a wonderful base fabric for a dress or the main part of a costume. Using the colors of the paisley, I chose other fabrics to accompany or complement the main fabric. The green polka-dot fabric would be a great choice for legs. Notice the textured silk pocket in the lower right-hand corner. The silk has a depth of color cotton fabric doesn't. Imagine it as a jacket or corset on the doll's costume.

The hand-dyed lace could decorate the hem of a dress or a pair of pantaloons. The darker green velvet at the bottom of the board adds wonderful color saturation and texture to the mix. Note how the trims are layered. While this layering is not always possible on a doll because of scale, it is interesting to see how the trims add visual interest and texture. One trim and a row of small beads may be more to scale, depending on the size of the doll.

The velvet flowers would be a fabulous accent at the waist or as a hat. Notice how they are shown with simple, hand-dyed rayon ribbon. The gold buttons and charms are not to scale, but you can bring those same gold tones to your costume with small charms, gold beads, or perhaps a buckle at the doll's waist.

Minidress

The main fabric of the minidress is the paisley print, which is complemented by the textural rose-colored velvet bodice. The hand-dyed lace adds a dimensional element. I have added an ecru apron with dark purple silk side flounces. I can visualize the green and white polka-dot legs from the color board and fancy shoes with gold buckles to complete the costume.

Keep an open mind when you are pulling out fabrics and trims for your doll project. It's better to start with more options than you will ultimately need and then carefully edit and eliminate to accomplish your goal. Once the materials are in front of you, you can have a blast mixing and matching, plotting and planning, to create a color palette for your doll.

Simply Elegant

This color board exudes elegance. The rose-colored French trim complements the main fabric selection, which is a simple cotton print with limited color variation, and provides welcome visual excitement. Velvet corners add depth and color saturation. Heat-set crystals add shimmer and sparkle. Using several shades of your central colors creates depth. Although the main fabric is simple in its color focus, it doesn't inhibit creative possibilities for a doll costume.

Minidress

This minidress is made from the main yellow print fabric. The bodice is made of the turquoise velvet, and the hem is accented with two layers of trim for an elegant feeling. The hand-dyed ribbon at the hips provides color variation as well as visual interest, as one color bleeds into the other. Maybe you can imagine deep mushroom-colored silk legs and rose-colored shoes, accented with sparkle crystals—I can!

Sail Away Style

This patriotic board shows how to accent with black and white for contrast. The familiar red, white, and blue theme is presented in this unusual way to show how the addition of black and white polka-dot corners and scroll trim create visual interest and contrast. Black and white accents can be added to almost any color combination for greater impact.

The floral print as the main fabric becomes more interesting when it is combined with black and white polka-dot fabric. The corners of the board feature velvet and silk ribbons as well as black and white scroll trim. Repeating the red, white, and blue theme in the trims and silk flowers pulls the whole combination together. You could trim the hem or bodice of a dress with a variety of similar trims and color combinations. Gold beads sewn or fused on trim create depth and sparkle. Use this technique around the hem edge of a skirt, dress, or pantaloons. Small ribbon flowers make the perfect waist, hem, or shoulder accent.

Minidress

The simple minidress unites the red, white, and blue theme with the pizzazz of the black and white check to stir up visual interest. The deep red velvet ribbon trim with gold beads down the center front provides the metal element that completes the look. Now this is just good fun, don't you agree?

Art Deco

This art deco color board illustrates how powerful a simple color scheme can be. The addition of black and white adds visual interest and the extra punch this color combination needs for excitement. The black lace layered over the periwinkle silk provides texture. The green polka-dot fabric adds visual variation, and the magenta ribbon conveys color depth and richness.

Minidress

On the minidress, the polka-dot fabric is used as the main costume fabric because the eye is drawn to the simple but noticeable polka-dot pattern. The solid periwinkle and burgundy silks complement the mossy green of the main fabric. The black lace enhances the simple color choices. Delicate trims follow the hemline and bodice for an extra visual treat. Mixing cotton with the laces and silks makes an exciting and varied color and textural presentation. I want a dress just like this one!

Consulting the Experts

I invited two of my favorite cloth doll artists to share their color boards with you. Elinor Peace Bailey and Patti Medaris Culea are accomplished cloth doll artists and have much to share with the cloth doll community. Their boards present what they have to say about their color worlds and sensibilities. I love the diversity of their art. The color palettes they work with are as unique to them as yours will be to you.

Color Board
By Elinor Peace Bailey

A complex display of fabric that leaves you breathless is what we're looking for here. Because the doll form lends itself to a painterly layering of color and texture, it is a grand home for excess—so I play with ruffles and flourishes, layers and transparencies, tiny details, and overall appearance. I never tire of seeing a completed form that has been spared nothing. To withhold some treasure will kill the piece. If using what you have is an excuse rather than a bragging point, then get better stuff! Like a magpie, collect what delights your eye from thrift stores, garage sales, quilt shops, and craft stores. A doll is a small object; she can hold a bit of the best.

I start with a complex color palette drawn from what I call a mother print, a main print from which everything else departs. I hope to find at least twelve colors in the mother print in order to have the greatest number of possibilities. Then I begin looking for things that sing when they are with that piece of fabric. I add until I am sated. Now, all of that pile might not be part of the finished piece, but it is all there for the audition. In this instance, I started with a vivid stripe and then grabbed as many textures as I could in about five minutes. I allow very little pondering time. Now, if you will excuse me, I am off to make a doll!

Color Board
By Patti Medaris Culea

Supposedly, eight percent of all men are colorblind, while just two percent of all women have that visual impairment. Perhaps this explains why guys sometimes don't appreciate the outfits that we think look spectacular.

I'm forever grateful that I'm among the 98 percent of women who identify colors. However, for me, it's much more than recognizing. I positively thrive on colors—especially yellows, pinks, greens, black, and white, which are those I work with the most. They are what I call my happy colors, and they brighten my day.

When I design a doll, the color of something as small as a scrap of fabric, a bead, or a piece of trim can greatly influence the finished creation. I'll see a new or unusual fabric and suddenly a doll will come to mind. I don't have a traditional color board in my head. For instance, I recently bought two fabrics. One had a yellow background with subtle polka dots in gold, while the other had pink, aqua, and black and white checks. The latter was used to create a new version of my Banbury Cross Beth doll pattern. She's at the center of the color board holding a book she's about to read. Butterflies were appliquéd along the border, and a beautiful white trim was added and then embellished with sequins and beads.

Mixing patterns is a fun approach. Forget the old rule to avoid clashing designs. I sometimes combine checks, stripes, polka dots, and a flower print to create a memorable doll. I then add lace, trim, and beadwork to complete my new friend. A motif, like the one on the top right, can be another exciting way to finish your doll.

Getting Started: Tools

Every art or craft requires tools. These are the tools I consider essential when I embark on a new doll project.

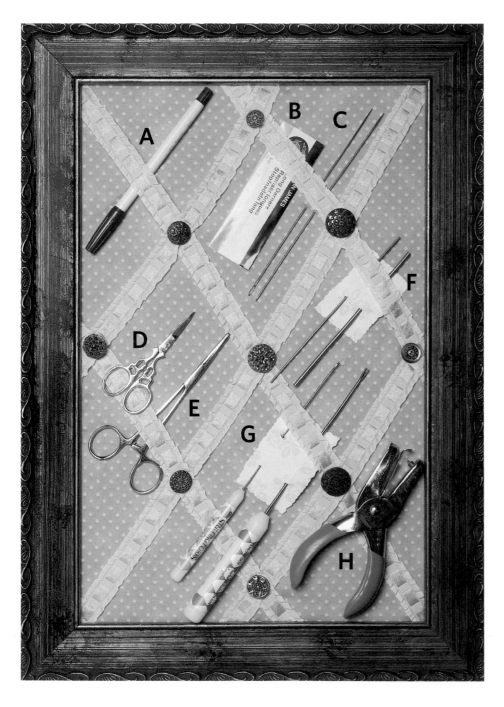

- **Purple fade-away marker (A)**
  Marks from this magic pen disappear completely. The color doesn't migrate to other parts of the doll.

- **John James long darner #7 needles (B)**
  These needles or an equivalent will make your soft sculpting a breeze. The needle is slim enough that it doesn't create holes in the fabric, flexible enough to move but retain its shape, and long enough to pass through all of my doll sculpting projects.

- **Jointing needles (C)**
  I prefer using 7" (17.8 cm) needles to string joint my dolls, but a 5" (12.7 cm) one will do as well. Keep two needles on hand if your doll is string jointed.

- **Small, sharp-point scissors (D)**
  Although it is nice to have scissors for both paper and fabric, it is an extra treat to have a small pair of very sharp scissors with pointed tips. They make the clipping and small cutting that is required much easier.

- **Hemostats (E)**
  These come in several sizes and types, with curved and straight tips. I prefer the straight tip ones and am inclined to have at least two sizes near me when I am making my dolls; a medium pair with a pointed tip for fingers and small areas, and a larger pair for stuffing wads of fiber fill into the doll parts.

Getting Started: Techniques

- **Brass turning tubes and steel rods for finger turning (F)**
  These are available commercially for cloth doll makers and usually come in a packet with three or four sizes of tubes in them. I create my own from small brass tubing, 1/8" (3 mm) and one size smaller 3/32" (2.4 mm) along with a small steel rod that will fit with a margin of ease into each tube. This type of tubing, and the steel rod is usually available at a hardware or hobby store.

- **Mini and Regular Stuffing Forks (G)**
  Available at several cloth doll making suppliers this is a must for stuffing your dolls. The mini is used primarily for the fingers, while the regular size is used for main cavities and limbs of the doll. Used in conjunction with the hemostats, your success is built in!

- **Hole punch (H)**
  Have regular hole punches at your finger tips when you need to punch a hole in your project. But, if you are in the mood to treat yourself, a Japanese screw punch will make short work through several layers and cuts clean every time.

Template-Method Sewing

To create simple pattern templates, copy the pattern pieces that start on page 110 (note that some patterns need to be enlarged; this can be done at a copy shop) onto card stock. The thickness of cardstock is perfect because it can be used over and over. By making actual cardstock patterns that you can trace, you will get perfect reproductions of the actual patterns. Carefully cut the pattern templates out in the middle of the black lines. Most body parts require that you trace the template onto fabric, sew on the traced line and then cut out the sewn pieces, in that order. General instructions follow and each project has specific instructions as well.

1. Fold the fabric with right sides together.

2. If the pattern piece has a straight-grain arrow, it is important to position it on the fabric so the arrow aligns with the straight grain (parallel to the selvage) of the fabric. This minimizes stretch and gives you a longer, leaner interpretation of the fabric pieces once they are stuffed. If the pattern piece does not have a straight-grain arrow, you can position it anywhere on the fabric.

3. Trace around the templates directly onto the folded fabric. If using light-colored fabrics, a mechanical pencil will give an exact reproduction of the pattern template. Trace lightly—just dark enough to see when you are sewing and not so dark that the lead is drawn into the fabric as you sew, which could cause a dark shadow along the seams.

   Trace the templates on dark fabric with a light gel pen. You can also use a purple fade-away fabric marker to trace the lower torso or legs and costume patterns, but make sure you sew shortly after you trace, before the ink disappears.

4. Sew directly on the traced line. Next, cut out the fabric about 1/4" (6 mm) outside the traced lines, unless otherwise noted, to create the seam allowance. In general, if you are using silk or another fabric that frays more than cotton, allow for just less than 1/2" (1.3 cm) seam allowance to guard against blown-out seams.

General Marking Guidelines

I learned a long time ago that the purple fade away markers are the best ones to use for cloth dolls. I generally use them to trace the torso, upper arms, and legs. I always use them on the faces to mark feature placement and to make the adjustment lines on the hands and fingers. Although the ink may take as much as a few days to fade away, it does eventually disappear.

I prefer to use the larger-tip marker rather than the fine-tip because it gives me a better mark and lines that generally last until I no longer need them.

Marking made with blue-ink water-soluble pens must be removed with water. When combined with fiberfill, the ink will migrate to portions of your doll's face, legs, and arms that you do not want when it dries. Even though you water away the marks on the nose, when the fabric dries you might find marks on the lips or cheek. This can last for several applications of water. I find this too frustrating and risky on the face because the water might make some inks run or leave stains over the powdered eye shadows and blushes used for facial coloration.

General Sewing Guidelines

- Start every project with a new sewing machine needle.

- Attach an open-toe appliqué presser foot. This makes sewing accurately along the traced lines infinitely easier.

- Set the machine to a short stitch, a 1.5 stitch length setting, or about 14 to 16 stitches per inch (2.5 cm) unless otherwise noted.

- Sew with cotton-wrapped polyester or 100 percent polyester thread; both are strong. Cotton thread is not strong enough for body construction; the seams might pop open with the pressure of the fiberfill.

Stitch Guide

Several basic stitches are used through the projects. Here are a few simple ones.

Ladder Stitch

This stitch is used to join two fabrics together along a fold. I often use this to attach a head to a neck when I do not want the stitches to show. The threads run directly across from each other in the fold of the fabric in groups of three or four stitches at one time. Then you pull the threads so the fabrics join together without the threads showing on the outside.

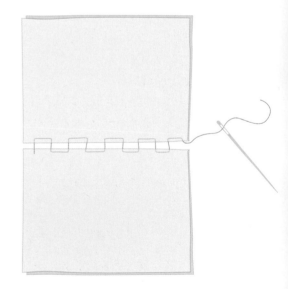

Ladder stitch

Burying the Tails of Thread

After I have stitched a closure and secured it with a knot I take the needle back into the fabric and bury the tails of thread inside the body part. The stitches will be more secure if you do not cut the threads at the knot. If you bury the thread tails, the knot will stay tied and your stitches will hold.

Bury the tails of the thread inside the arm.

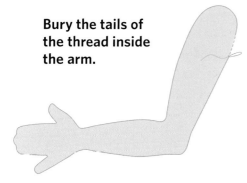

Running Stitch

A basic running stitch is used throughout the projects to gather edges of fabric. Use heavy thread and sew this stitch in a straight line with space between the stitches.

Running stitch

General Stuffing Techniques

Stuffing is one of the most important techniques for making a nice doll. The stuffing must be evenly distributed for a smooth and lump-free surface. The size of the doll, the type of stuffing you use, and your stuffing technique are all relevant variables.

There are two basic types of polyester fiberfill. One is fast-compacting and wads easily. The other has a slippery, lofty feel. I prefer the latter sort, which has a silicone finish that keeps it from compacting too quickly. I like the option of adding extra stuffing and having it meld into the existing stuffing instead of creating a bump, as the fast-compacting types often do. Several brands with this lofty, slippery finish are available, including Fairfield's Soft Touch Supreme.

I also recommend three tools to help you do the job:

- A pair of straight-nose hemostats for placing small or large wads of stuffing in a specific area.

- A mini stuffing fork for fingers and small areas.

- A regular stuffing fork for general stuffing purposes.

Specific Stuffing Techniques

As a general rule, work with large wads of stuffing to fill large cavities. Fewer pieces of stuffing make a much smoother-looking finished piece. Little wads, unless you are doing a hand or other small area, could appear lumpy.

To stuff all but the hands and other small areas, take a sizable wad of stuffing and poke it into the cavity with your fingers. Then start compacting the stuffing in the center of the wad as you poke it into the cavity. Only use a stuffing fork to compact the stuffing at the bone location in a limb. Do not pounce all along the surface or on top of the exposed stuffing; rather, feed it only to the center with the fork or hemostats. If you keep the top of the wad of stuffing lofty, it will meld in with the next piece you feed, making similar textures. If you pounce the stuffing on top to compact it, you change the texture of the stuffing so it is no longer lofty but rather hard and flat. These two textures will never meld, and the transition from one piece of stuffing to the next will be obvious on the limb and the surface of the fabric skin. Think of stuffing like stacking paper cups: You add one cup at a time to gradually build a tall stack of cups. Add large wads of stuffing, compact them to the center, and add another piece of stuffing on top so it nestles into the hole in the center until the limb or torso is filled as desired.

I generally use only a mini stuffing fork for the fingers and a regular stuffing fork and hemostats for the rest of the doll.

Stuffing a Leg

This shows how to stuff a leg to keep the ankle stable and create a nice texture. Notice how the first wad of stuffing fills the foot but leaves the heel vacant, and how the next wad comes halfway up the lower leg. This keeps the ankle from bending, unless it is a very large doll. The direction the stuffing is added acts almost as an armature at the ankle. Continue stuffing to the top of the leg. The stuffing should be firm and full without being rock-hard, which would stress the seams.

Stuffing the Torso

To stuff a main cavity, like the torso, use a regular stuffing fork and a pair of hemostats to compact and manipulate the stuffing.

To stuff an upper torso from a bottom opening, use large wads of stuffing. First, compact stuffing into the neck until it is very firm, and then fill most of the torso. After the torso is mostly full, use the hemostats to add a large wad of stuffing to each shoulder to keep the shoulders full. The added wads of stuffing will lie on top of the existing stuffing, and fill the vacant shoulder areas. Continue to stuff the lower torso to the hips and then add the legs, or continue as the instructions direct.

To stuff an upper torso through a neck opening, feed the stuffing in with a regular stuffing fork in a steady stream of stuffing. I like to tuck the torso under my arm and hold the neck opening with one hand as I feed the fiberfill with my other hand and the stuffing fork.

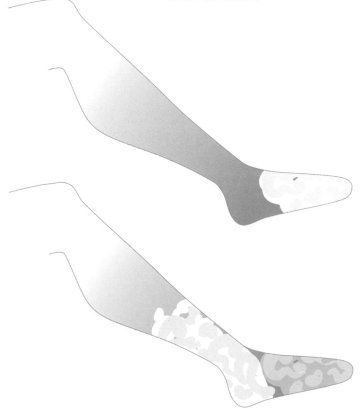

Stuffing the Hands

Hands are an important statement for a doll; they are expressive and always visible, so they must look nice. Your doll should not have to wear gloves to cover a bad stuffing job.

Most of my dolls hands have wires in the fingers. I stuff only the top of each finger on top of the wire, using a mini stuffing fork and a small amount of stuffing.

Lay the mini stuffing fork in the ditch between your two fingers, over the stuffing. Hold the fork with your thumb. Rotate the fork around and around evenly in one direction. The fork will grab and load a long, even tube of stuffing.

Guide the loaded stuffing fork up into the arm and then into the finger on top of the wire. As you move into the arm and hand, do not pull back with the fork, or the stuffing will come off the fork and you will have to fish it out with the hemostats.

Hold the finger from the outside and pull the fork out. The stuffing will fill the finger nicely and evenly. Practice makes perfect here. You will get better at judging how much stuffing to use for each finger. There is no need to stuff the bottom side of the wire on the fingers; this tends to overfill the fingers and serves no purpose. Once the fingers are stuffed, I use the hemostats to finish filling the top and

palm of the hand. Be careful not to overfill the hands, or they will be puffy. Add just enough stuffing to sandwich the wires between the top and bottom.

I do not wind stuffing onto the fork for the main cavity or limb stuffing. Instead, I use the fork to poke down the stuffing—to the center, like bones. So although the winding technique is great for the fingers, I don't recommend it for the main parts of the doll because it compacts and alters the texture of the stuffing.

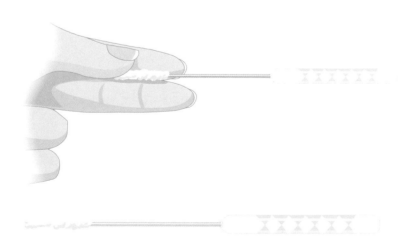

Stuffing Forks

# Creating Gabriella
A Flat and Fabulous
Two-Dimensional Cloth Doll

Flat dolls open the door to creative expression. They offer an enticing and accessible approach to cloth doll making. Unlike their close relative, the paper doll, flat cloth dolls include the tactile element that only fibers provide. Fabric makes us want to touch as part of the experience. Our eyes tell us one thing, but our hands tell us another.

Everyone can create a cloth doll! I invite you to join me and create a cloth doll of your own. Find your inspiration as you make all kinds of doll figures on which to lavish your stash of fabric, trims, and ribbons.

Early fashion plates from the 1700s through the 1800s are the inspiration for my flat cloth doll art. European fashion houses employed artists to bring life to the couture designer's creations. These lovely illustrations were published in magazines for refined ladies so they could learn about current fashions. The images offer inspiration for both vintage and new textiles. Here, a vintage figure from the early 1800s is used as the model for Gabriella.

Combining vintage images, laces, ribbons, trims, and buttons with vintage textiles offers eclectic choices for designing art dolls. This approach offers a second debut for all things vintage, making old things new and new things old.

Endless exciting materials are available to experiment with and explore. Beautiful fabrics, but also fabulous rubber stamps, metal charms, metallic threads, bonded fiber papers that act like fabric, gold leafing pens, fiber dyes, and fabric sheets that run through ink-jet printers await our creative touch. Although some of the techniques used here are not in themselves innovative, they are all exciting, creative,

and artistic. Anything is new if you have never done it before.

As you visit the gallery of flat cloth dolls you will be inspired by how vibrant this art can be. All of the gallery artists were given the vintage image on page 111 to work with. No rules or guidelines were issued except "Make her pretty." The artists were asked to let their imagination guide them in creating their version of a flat cloth doll. All I can say is "Wow!," and I know you will too.

Join me, and I will guide you, step by step, through the process of creating Gabriella. Let's make art!

Creating Gabriella

MATERIALS

- 1–2 colorfast fabric ink-jet sheets in cream or white
- ½ yard (30.5 cm) dupioni silk for skirt
- ¼ yard (22.9 cm) coordinating small-print, cotton fabric for the backing
- small piece of black silk for the corset
- trims, beads, assorted silk flowers for skirt and headdress
- lace for sleeves and corset trim
- small trims and ribbon for the upper corset and sleeves
- small buttons and beads
- silk flowers and/or velvet leaves
- medium tassel for bottom of the dress
- small tassel for bottom of the corset
- ½ yard (45.7 cm) narrow cord
- small piece of fusible stabilizer, such as Timtex or Peltex
- heavyweight iron-on fusible web, such as HeatnBond
- matching threads
- heavy nylon upholstery thread
- tacky glue
- spray art fixative, such as Krylon
- aqua, dark gray, lavender, peach, and rose colored pencils
- white gel pen
- black Pigma pen, 005 tip, such as Sakura Micron Pigma Pen
- rubber stamps
- pigment or fabric stamp pads
- 1–3 pieces of ½-yard (30.5 cm) cuts of ½–1" (1.3-2.5 cm) ribbon to embellish tassel

TOOLS

- ink-jet printer
- sewing machine
- flat, stiff brush, ½" (1.3 cm) wide, with fairly short bristles
- 9" × 12" (22.9 x 30.5 cm) piece of poster board
- wooden craft stick
- iron
- straight pins
- hand needle
- small pair of sharp fine-tip fabric scissors
- paper scissors
- measuring tape
- clear ruler or hem gauge
- tape
- purple fade-away marking pen
- small hole punch

Getting Started

Read the instructions completely before you start. This will get your creative juices flowing, help you plan your project, and give you a sense of order.

When using an existing illustration, like we are using here, keep in mind that it might need adjustment to suit your personal vision. I have made a few changes to the pose by cutting and repositioning the arms and cutting off the skirt. I also enlarged the image to make it easier for you to work with.

⑤ Cut out the images to create two figures. On the first image, cut away the arms, leaving the upper part of the sleeve intact. Throw the arms away. Then trim the torso and cut away the skirt and hair as shown (**B**).

Creating the Paper Torso

① Make a good color copy of the double image found on page 111 using a color copy machine.

② Adjust the color of your ink-jet printer as necessary so you can transfer the image onto fabric. Load the paper tray with a colorfast fabric sheet and make one copy of the double image. Follow the manufacturer's instructions to heat-set the color on the colorfast fabric sheet.

③ Turn over the double image and fuse a piece of iron-on fusible web to cover the entire back. Remove the paper backing and fuse a piece of poster board onto the back of the images. Fuse a second piece of iron-on fusible web to the blank side of the poster board.

④ Cut out an 8½" × 11" (21.6 × 27.9 cm) piece of small-print cotton fabric. Remove the paper backing from the back of the poster board and fuse the fabric to the board. The poster board will be sandwiched between the images on one side and the small-print fabric on the other (**A**).

6. On the second image, cut the arms off at an angle as shown. Cut out the arms and hands carefully. Trim away the ruffled part of the sleeve. Loosely cut away the head so it forms a square block (**C**).

7. Apply tacky glue along the upper sleeve area of the first image. Position the angled cut arms on top of the glue and away from the body a bit. This allows room to place the skirt around the waist area later. Let the glue set (**D**).

8. Cut out a small block of Timtex and glue it to the back of the square head image. Cut out the same size square of the small-print fabric and glue it to the back of the Timtex on the head.

9. Use a gray pencil to lightly define the chin and jaw line on the front of the image and create a cutting line. The chin is not shaded well on the image, so your line will determine the actual chin and jaw line (**E**).

10. Carefully cut out the head image around the hair, flowers, and chin and jaw line. This is the face you will color. Dab the cut edges with tacky glue to keep them from fraying. Let the glue dry.

11. Cut the wooden craft stick to 3–4" (7.6–10.2 cm) long. Apply glue to one side of the stick and place it on the back of the doll from the head to the lower spine to reinforce her neck.

12. Cut a strip of the small-print cotton fabric and glue it in place to cover the stick. You can reinforce the arms the same way, if you like.

Detailing the Facial Features and Finishing the Head

① Blush the cheeks to a rosy glow with colored pencils. I applied the colored pencil and then softened the color with a flat, stiff brush.

② Color the eyelids with a soft colored pencil in lavender, aqua, or peach.

③ Enhance the outline of the eyes with the 005 tip black Pigma pen.

④ Enhance the whites of the eyes with the white gel pen.

⑤ Color in the lips with a colored pencil.

⑥ Spray fixative to set the color. Let it dry. (It's best to do this outside.)

⑦ Apply glue to the back of the painted head. Press the head in place over the other head. This second head will add depth and create visual interest.

⑧ Glue silk flowers to the head to create the headdress.

TIP

I used three stamps and three stamp-pad colors to create the skirt.

Creating the Skirt

① Measure and cut a 14" × 36–40" (35.6 × 91.4–101.6 cm) piece of pastel silk dupioni. Lay out the silk on a clean flat surface, right side up.

② Create texture and visual pattern interest on the fabric with rubber stamps and pigment stamp pads. Use more than one stamp style and more than one color stamp pad. Apply the stamping in a random pattern.

③ Heat-set the stamping with a dry iron.

④ Measure and mark the placement of the trims you selected with a measuring tape or hem gauge and a purple fade-away marking pen.

⑤ Glue or stitch the trims, beads, buttons, charms, and other embellishments to the skirt fabric as desired. Do not attach anything too close to the bottom edge of the skirt because it is gathered later, and you want to see the trims.

⑥ Fold the skirt panel in half, right sides together, to create a center back seam. Machine-stitch the seam.

⑦ Using a single length of heavy nylon upholstery thread, hand-sew a running stitch along the top and bottom edges. The stitching at the top (waist) should be a generous ¼" (6 mm) from the raw edge, and the bottom (hem edge) stitching should be about 1" (2.5 cm) from the raw edge. Leave long tails of thread at each end. Don't knot the thread.

⑧ Turn the skirt right-side out and set it aside (**F**).

F

Making the Corset

1. Make a copy of the torso pattern on page 110. Cut out carefully on the line to create the pattern template.

2. Adhere fusible web to one side of a small piece of poster board that is 1" (2.5 cm) larger all around than the torso pattern template.

3. On the blank side (no fusible web) of the posterboard, trace the torso pattern and cut it out exactly on the line.

4. Remove the paper backing from the fusible web and fuse a piece of black silk that is larger than the torso to the poster board. Cut the fabric, leaving a ¼" (6 mm) margin all around the torso pattern.

5. Clip notches in the fabric, up to the poster board, all around the corset as shown (**G**). Run a thin ribbon of glue around the back edge of the poster board. Press the raw edges of the fabric securely to the back.

6. Glue narrow trim down the center front of the corset. Glue additional trim along the top and bottom edges as desired.

7. Cut a strip of a fine lace, 10–15" (25.4–38.1 cm) long × 2" (5.1 cm) wide.

G

8. Sew a running stitch along the top edge of the lace strip with heavy nylon thread and no knots. Pull the threads to gather the lace.

9. Turn the corset over and run a bead of tacky glue along the bottom edge of the back.

10. Lay the gathered edge of the lace along the glued edge, evenly distributing the gathers.

11. Gather an additional piece of lace to tuck along the inside top edge of the corset; glue it in place. Alternatively, glue a piece of lace directly along the top edge of the doll's chest to cover the lacy portion of the illustration.

12. Sew or glue buttons down the center front of the corset. Embellish as desired.

13. Sew the small tassel to the bottom tip of the corset and set the corset aside.

Making the Sleeves

1. Cut 2 pieces of fine lace to 2½ × 7–8" (6.4 × 17.8–20.3 cm).

2. Fold 1 piece of lace in half, right sides together, and stitch by machine or by hand as you did the skirt's back seam. Repeat for the other piece of lace. Turn the pieces right side out.

3. Hand-sew a running stitch along the top edge of the sleeve with heavy nylon thread and no knot. Leave long tails of thread.

4. Hand-sew a second running stitch, ½" (1.3 cm) from the bottom of the sleeve edge, to create the sleeve ruffle.

5. Slide the sleeves onto the arms. Pull the threads to gather, and tighten the sleeve to the arm. First arrange the top gathers, and then the bottom gathers. Dab the top of the sleeve with tacky glue to secure the sleeves.

6. Tie a small ribbon or cord around the lower sleeves to decorate.

Assembling the Doll

1. Use a small hole punch to punch a hole in the lower torso as shown.

2. String an 18–20" (45.7–50.8 cm) length of cord or strong ribbon through the front of the hole to the back. Tie a knot in the top of the cord, and tape it to the torso to secure (**H**).

3. Pull the skirt up onto the doll's waist. Tie the tails of the heavy nylon thread to gather it tight, leaving the raw edges up. Tie a secure knot on the back. Trim all excess raw threads from the waist and trim down the fabric as small as possible. Dab the waist with glue to hold the skirt on securely. Wrap a piece of ½" (1.3 cm) wide ribbon around the waist like a waistband. Tie it in a bow in the back to cover the raw edges of the top of the skirt. Dab glue on the ribbon to hold it in place.

4. Glue the corset over the torso, covering the raw skirt threads.

5. Pull the tails of the thread on the bottom of the skirt to gather it; the cord should be hanging out the bottom of the skirt.

6. Loop the cord through the tassel, pull it up, and knot or tape it at the right length. The tassel should extend to the bottom of the skirt without any of the cord showing.

H

7. Pull the gathering threads at the bottom of the skirt, poking the raw edges to the inside as you tighten it around the top of the tassel.

8. Tie extra lengths of ribbon into bows around the top of the tassel.

9. Cut pieces of lace, trim, or even velvet leaves to create epaulets for the shoulders. Glue them in place to cover the point where the sleeves end.

10. Sew a small ribbon loop or a small brass ring to the back of the doll's head so you can hang her on the wall to admire her and show her off!

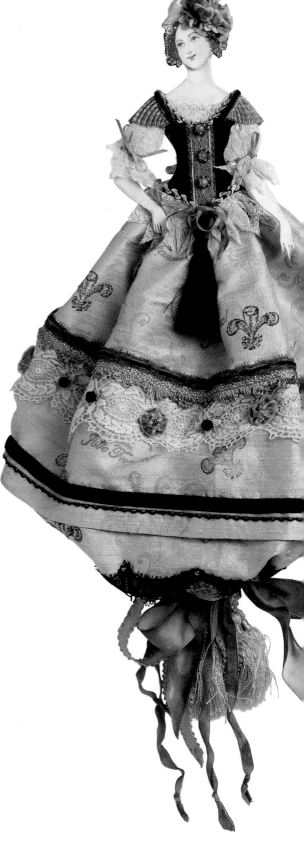

Gallery

Mermaid
by Arley Berryhill

To make this vintage-looking mermaid, the original body was cut off at the waist to add the tail and fins. The arms where repositioned to fit with the underwater pose. After backing the whole piece with fusible Peltex, I covered the body in green velvet. On top of the velvet I added overlapping pieces of hand-painted Venice lace. I hand-dyed the lace with Dyna Flow paints and then stitched it into place using free-motion embroidery with variegated rayon threads.

I made the tail and side fins with several layers of gathered iridescent chiffons, stitched down in a fanlike design using free-motion stitches. After I embroidered the fins with beads, I added a layer of thread fringe. I put more lace on the edges to blend into the body, and I added painted velvet leaves to the tail fin.

I made the purple and pink thread fringe on the fins by free-motion stitching on thick dissolvable stabilizer (Solvy brand). I built up layers of threads on the Solvy, using several colors of variegated and metallic threads. Stitching horizontally across the top edge of the fringe keeps the threads together after the stabilizer is washed away. I also used free-motion fringe to make the pink hair and the green and pink seaweed sleeves.

I cut up and assembled gold metallic lace, painted green, to form the headdress and to trim the neckline and gloves. I decorated the neckline and gloves with gathered chiffon ribbon.

Masquerade
by Judy Brown

My challenge technique for this doll was "Vintage Flair." What comes to my mind when I think of vintage is the fashions worn in the 1930s, '40s and '50s. I decided she would wear a costume of pink and black, maybe in polka dots, sport fishnet hose, and carry a black mask. I changed most of the original image, except for her pose.

I copied the original face and a new body shape onto the white fabric sheet. I then ironed this onto Peltex with a fabric backing. Next, I stitched the polka-dot fabric to her skirt. I used black machine stitching to simulate fishnet hose and then shaded it with a black pencil. I used pink silk for her bodice and stitched lace to her upper arms and elbows. I made her jointed at the elbows, so when you move her arm you can either see her face or hide it with the mask.

I ironed black silk dupioni to a stabilizer and then cut it into points. I stitched these under the bodice and then embellished with tiny silver pompoms, which I also attached to the toes of her shoes. Her hair and shoes are painted with black acrylic paint. I used vintage pink crepe paper for her collar and hat trim. I trimmed the hem of her skirt in black tulle, which I also used for the pompoms on her bodice and the tip of her hat.

Courtesan of Versailles
by Betts Vidal

I love a project that begins with a provided image and has only a few requirements. My instructions were to include something old, something new, something pretty … and whatever I created should reflect both my art and me. I couldn't wait to get started!

I challenged myself by creating this doll's costume with materials I already had. No late-night trips to the fabric store for a specific trim or trinket. For me, that's a challenge.

While searching through my overabundant stash of fabrics, ribbons, and trinkets, I came across this wide pea-green ribbon with black borders. This inspired me to dress her entirely in ribbon. I imagined her gown to be a ribbon lattice. After trimming off the black borders and folding the remaining green area, I wove it and attached it to a firm art board. What appear to be several overskirts are simply folds of the untrimmed ribbon. Her sleeves were the next challenge.

A vintage black velvet ribbon worked for her sleeves, and a new pleated velvet ribbon became her peplum and regal collar. While playing with other colored ribbons to complement the green, I finally realized that black is the complement

The gown is a compilation of ribbons by Vidal, Offray, and Mokuba.

An ornate gold metal piece originally designed as a book corner enhances her décolletage. To repeat the gold, I added treasured mirror-back buttons from my vintage collection. Snippets of ribbon appear between the layered loops, and a petite silk ribbon became her choker, along with a black crystal. Pea-green beads (a lucky find) sewn onto her woven gown and along her sleeves satisfied my compelling desire to bead just about everything.

After laboring over what to do with her shoulders, I came across the ribbon edge trimmings. Perfect! The wired edges helped form delicate bows that act as epaulets. (Think twice before tossing any trimmings, no matter how small!) In an add-just-one-more-thing moment, I added a Victorian passementerie. Behold—a courtesan of Versailles.

Australia
by Gloria McKinnon

Dolls, both porcelain and cloth, have long been a source of fascination for me. It gives me great joy to combine elegant decoration, embellishment, and embroidery with the notion of a stylish flat doll.

I love to use the print as my canvas and fabulous silk ribbons and threads as my palette.

From the print Barbara sent me, I created a beautiful journal cover or needle book cover. On further thought, I realized this piece also could be exquisitely framed for the wall or used as the main feature of a wall hanging, supplemented with more lace and sumptuous fabrics.

I first imagined the doll in a garden, but her elegance dictated a stage setting. In creating her, I incorporated basic embroidery stitches using single strands of fine silk to enhance the lace and folds of her skirt, silk ribbon embroidery to embellish the flowers on her beautiful dress, and hand-dyed lace for extra dimension and subtlety in the stage curtains. I love to use beads to add depth and sparkle and to make a setting really special.

The final luxury is a stunning bow of bias-cut silk satin ribbon that holds the journal closed, so one will wonder at the treasures within. Remember, more is never enough!

Marie Antoinette
by Ulla Milbrath

When I saw the doll Barbara sent me, I instantly thought of Marie Antoinette! I wanted an old-fashioned French color palette and decided on pink, brown, and tan.

First, I cut out a basic bell-like skirt shape for my doll from a beautiful Spencerian flourish paper. Then, I looked through my boxes of fabrics, papers, and ribbons for samples of my chosen colors. A wonderful brown rose-trellis ribbon seemed perfect for the center of her dress. The original Spencerian flourish underskirt was completely covered by the time I finished—except for the piece just under her hand, pointing down. I hadn't planned on adding the music-paper panier, but I felt the skirt needed something to hold it together.

I made the blouse from a lovely bright pink tie-dyed silk ironed onto fabric. I then added hand-painted silk flower petals for the sleeves and music-paper cuffs. For her hair, I needle-felted white wool roving on top of a piece of white felt. I love the realistic look it gives. I then sewed on the ribbons, trim, and pearls and added feathers on top.

The golden bough was an afterthought. She needed something to hold. I fiddled around with some gold Dresden antlers and came up with a branchlike shape I liked. The idea of Marie holding court with a golden bough in hand appeals to my romantic sensibilities.

Shelly C. Mermaid
by Sharon Martin

I had previously made a pretty, flat fiber clamshell for another doll and was unable to use it for that project; it was too small for the doll it was made for and too large to be just an accessory for another doll. Boy, this is sounding a lot like the Three Bears. I wanted to make a doll for my clamshell that was just right. The instructions for this challenge were simple enough, just "keep her pretty." So the prim and proper Victorian lady morphed into a mermaid, just right for my clamshell.

I painted the tail with a base coat of dark green and a top coat of gold, blotting some of the gold off before it dried. I wanted her to look as if she had scales like a fish. I put small scales of glue on her tail and sprinkled vintage glass glitter on them. She needed a pretty bodice fiber with a bit of dimension. My mind went immediately to a recent purchase I had made of beautiful hand-dyed lace. The colors of the lace were perfect for my clamshell, so I used the lace on the bodice as well as on the tail fins.

I wanted to find a better transition from the beautiful lace on the fins and the gold paint on the rest of the tail. I checked my stash of yarn and found one that matched the lace colors. I started just above the lace and wrapped the tail with yarn. Then I unwrapped most of the yarn in a change of direction and left only a small band by the top of the lace.

I was still feeling she wanted more interest and dimension. I dug through my suitcase of beads and chose beads for her tail and hair. She is from the sea, after all, so she needed a few shells to make her seaworthy and complete. There she was, finally ready for her debut under the sea—Shelly C. Mermaid.

The Gypsy Fortune-Teller
by Pamela Armas

My challenge was a pretty face and the desire to create a gypsy fortune-teller I remembered from my childhood. I spread my "Treasures of the Gypsy" stash of opulent fabrics, ribbons, trims, appliqués, and beads on my work surface, ready to be cut, gathered, and stitched into a creation reminiscent of fond memories and childhood play. Orange has always been this gypsy's favorite color, so bits and pieces of orange treasure and fabrics just seemed to come forward.

The gypsy's skirts are layers of silk and rayon fabrics gathered and beaded to create tucks and folds where bottles of secret potions and amulet charms are hidden.

Hand-dyed crinkle silk was fused to a heavyweight Peltex to create a strong foundation for the gypsy's underskirt, which holds the tools of her trade: tarot cards, charms, amulets, and secret symbols. To strengthen this foundation, larger beads were whip-stitched around the edges so she would be freestanding in order to exercise her rituals.

To create the mini tarot cards, I reduced a standard set of tarot cards to 1" × 2" (2.5 × 5.1 cm). Next, I fused these images to a jacquard silk fabric ink-jet sheet backed with wool felt, stitched around the perimeter, and then beaded all the edges.

I made the gypsy's tambourine from parchment paper, antique-painted metal sequins, and a tiny antique braid. I sewed seed beads, appliqués, and trims all over the costume for that special gypsy sparkle! Wrapped around her arm is the gypsy's snake, which I hand-painted onto fabric and fused to a silk fabric ink-jet sheet. Over eighty ringlets of iridescent seed bead loops make up her hair.

The Gypsy Fortune-Teller dances across my studio. I can feel magic in the air!

3 Creating Jolie
A Basic Cloth Doll with a Full-Color Face

Jolie is a wonderful cloth doll that lets you explore the process of making a three-dimensional figure. Human proportion is not necessary to capture the whimsy and creative expression of a cloth doll. Although I prefer to give my dolls some likeness to human proportion, I am inclined to let them have fantasy proportions for an imaginary and creative purpose.

Two ways to create cloth doll faces are explained in this chapter. If you are new to cloth doll making, try the full-color face transfer (page 112), which is ready for you to copy onto a cream or ivory-colored fabric transfer sheet on your ink-jet printer or at a copy shop. If you are eager to learn how to draw and color your own facial details, just follow the step-by-step instructions.

Cloth dolls lend themselves to a playful approach to creativity; they are not bound by traditions or prerequisites. The cloth doll making journey is limited by nothing more than your own creative spirit. My desire is to share my journey and help you discover the cloth doll maker in you. Making a cloth doll is all about the process, the fun of sewing, and the serendipitous creativity that occurs along the way.

As does every craft and art, the doll making process features a learning curve. Allow yourself to enjoy the learning, and don't focus solely on the outcome. I have tossed many a body part in the round file with no regrets. I have a name for these early attempts: precursors to excellence. This attitude lets me play and experiment without fear of failing or fear of not achieving perfection the first time. The creation process is the joy.

My Jolie doll is just another excuse to pull out the delicious heaps of fabrics, trims, laces, and buttons I so love. The lure of my stash is motivation enough for me to make a doll.

I begin as always by piling fabrics and trims on the table in front of me. From these I create an informal color board and audition fabrics for Jolie's costume. I am looking for a fabric that suits my mood and direction. You should pick a main fabric with enough color or pattern that all the other fabrics, trims, and accents can spin off it. Use top-quality fabrics and fiberfill for the doll body, as discussed in chapter 1. Remember that it's better to start with more; you can eliminate as you go. Jolie has cotton legs, face, and hands; however, her torso and upper arms are dupioni silk.

Jolie is my personal version of this doll pattern. I invite you to re-create her—or, better yet, be inspired by her to create your own version.

Creating Jolie

MATERIALS

It is best to be prepared by having everything you need to create your doll on hand before you begin. Many of the supplies listed are items you already have, but some are doll-specific. The Internet is a useful tool for sourcing fabrics and supplies.

- 3–4 pieces heavy paper or card stock for template
- ⅓ yard (30.5 cm) silk or cotton fabric for the torso
- ⅓ yard (30.5 cm) fabric for the legs
- ¼ yard (22.9 cm) ivory cotton fabric for the hands, lower arms, and head/face
- ⅓ yard (30.5 cm) silk fabric for the upper arms and head wrap
- ⅓ yard (30.5 cm) fabric for the skirt and bodice
- ⅓ yard (30.5 cm) silk fabric for the pantalets
- ¼ yard (22.9 cm) silk fabric for the puff sleeves
- 7" × 4" (17.8 × 10.2 cm) lace fabric for the lace sleeves
- 8" (20.3 cm) piece of ½" (1.3 cm) lace for the ruff
- remnants of soft, thin leather or Ultrasuede for shoes in two colors
- laces, trims, buttons, velvet flowers, and ribbons
- hair fiber—mohair, mohair yarn, Tibetan, or other
- cotton-wrapped polyester threads to match the fabrics
- bag of fiberfill, such as Fairfield's Soft Touch Supreme
- heavy nylon thread
- cream or ivory fabric sheet for ink-jet printer (optional)
- white and pastel green or blue gel pens
- white acrylic paint
- 4 chenille stems
- black, blue, green, and brown Pigma pens, 005 or 01 tip, such as Sakura Micron Pigma Pens
- colored pencils, two lip colors and a dark gray

- 1½ yards (13.7 m) of 1" (2.5 cm) ribbon for trim
- powdered, colored eye shadows and blushes
- spray art fixative, such as Krylon
- tacky glue

OPTIONAL

- 8" × 20–40" (20.3 × 50.8-101.6 cm) lace for skirt/apron
- ⅓ yard (30.5 cm) each of two colors dupioni silk for side flounces

TOOLS

- sharp scissors
- sewing machine
- open-toe appliqué presser foot
- straight pins
- hand needles
- 5-7" (12.7-17.8 cm) doll needle
- brass turning tube and rod, ⅛" (3 mm)
- straight-nose hemostats
- stuffing forks, regular and mini sizes
- iron
- ink-jet printer
- 6" (15.2 cm) metal hem gauge with slide indicator
- makeup sponge wand applicators
- short liner brush to apply eye shadow
- mechanical pencil
- purple fade-away fabric marking pen
- small paintbrush

Getting Started

Read through the project to get a good overview of the steps before starting the doll. This will help you visualize what lies ahead and collect your materials in advance.

Prepare all the pattern templates for Jolie (pages 112–118). The patterns include torso, arm, leg, head front, head back, pantalets, shoe, shoe spat, and flounce. Lay them out on the chosen fabrics and refer to the instructions for template-method sewing (page 25).

Creating the Torso

① Choose a solid or small-print fabric with no stretch for the torso. Jolie's torso is made from a dark brown dupioni silk. Fold the torso fabric in half, right sides together. Lay the torso pattern on top so the straight grain arrow is parallel to the selvage. Trace around the pattern.

② Set your sewing machine for a 1.5 stitch length and sew directly on the traced line, except for the bottom edge. Cut out the torso, leaving a ¼" (6 mm) seam allowance (½" [1.3 cm] if using silk fabric) all around. Do not clip any curves.

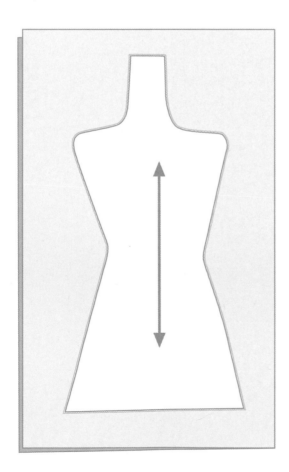

Creating the Legs

① Choose a tightly woven fabric that doesn't stretch for the legs. It doesn't have to be a skin color; a small print or colored solid looks great.

② Fold the leg fabric in half, right sides together, and trace two legs, allowing at least 1" (2.5 cm) between them. Stitch both legs directly on the lines, leaving the tops of both legs unstitched.

③ Cut out the legs, leaving a generous ¼" (6 mm) allowance for the seams. But cut directly on the line across the top. Turn the legs right side out and stuff them firmly up to the knees (see page 28).

④ Knot a double length of thread and sew through the knee from the back seam to the front seam. (**A**) Wrap the thread around the knee tightly two or three times to shape it. (**B**) Knot the thread securely and bury the thread tails in the leg. Repeat on the remaining leg.

⑤ Stuff the upper part of each leg, leaving a slight gap directly above the knee so the legs bend easily. Stuff to within 1" (2.5 cm) of the top and whipstitch the legs closed so the seams meet.

⑥ Pin the legs to the torso back as shown and stitch them in place by machine (**C**).

⑦ Pin and whipstitch the center crotch closed and then from the center crotch out to one side. This attaches one leg completely to the torso but leaves one leg open so you can finish stuffing the torso. Finish stuffing, and then whipstitch the remaining leg to the torso.

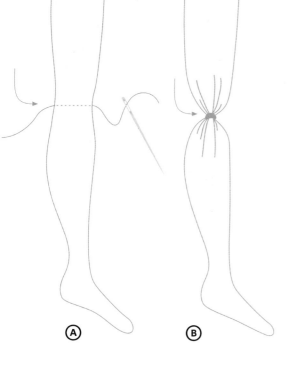

Ⓐ   Ⓑ

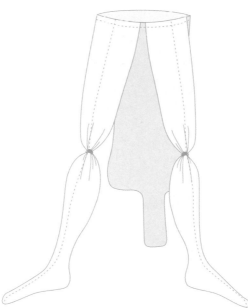

Ⓒ

Creating the Arms and Hands

The following directions explain how to make a wired elbow and a hand with fingers and a thumb. However, you can skip the finger detail and still have a lovely hand. Just stuff the mitt and thumb with fiberfill and stuff the arm as directed below, skipping the wired elbow.

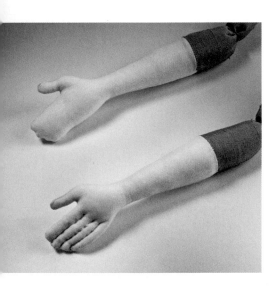

① Cut a piece of ivory-colored fabric to 5" × 12" (12.7 × 30.5 cm) for the lower arms and hands. Cut a piece of print or solid-colored fabric for the upper arms to 8" × 12" (20.3 × 30.5 cm).

② Pin the lower arm/hand fabric to the upper arm fabric along a long edge, right sides together. Stitch with a ¼" (6 mm) seam allowance. Press the seam allowance toward the upper arm fabric.

③ Fold the seamed fabric with right sides together. Trace the arm template twice, so the upper arm is on the colorful or print fabric and the lower arm and hand are on the ivory fabric. The dotted line on the pattern should be directly over the fabric seam. Use a light mechanical pencil around the hand section and a fade-away fabric pen or light-colored gel pen around the arm section. Leave at least ½" (1.3 cm) between the traced arms for seam allowances.

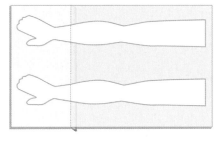

④ Stitch on the traced lines, leaving the tops of the arms unstitched. As your stitching approaches the V between the thumb and the mitt, take two stitches straight across at the base as shown. This makes it possible to clip the seam so it will turn smoothly and lie flat.

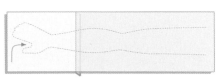

TIP

Turning tubes are helpful for creating lovely hands. I made my own turning tube from a 6" (15.2 cm) piece of ⅛" (3 mm) -diameter brass tubing and a small steel rod. These tubes are commercially available as well, as noted in the resources section (page 126).

⑤ Cut around the stitching, leaving a ¼" (6 mm) seam allowance around the arm and ⅛" (3 mm) around the mitt and thumb. Clip between the thumb and mitt very close to the stitching, as shown.

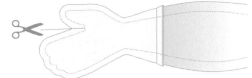

⑥ Insert the brass tube inside the arm into the thumb and use the rod to press the tip of the thumb firmly against the tube opening. Roll the thumb fabric up onto the rod to turn the thumb. Reach inside the mitt with the hemostats to turn the hand/arm right side out.

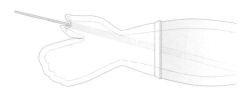

⑦ Mark the finger details on the mitt part of the hand with a purple fade-away fabric marking pen. Hand- or machine-stitch the finger details. I much prefer to do this step by hand with a single knotted thread.

⑧ Cut chenille stems to size as needed to wire the fingers. Crimp back ⅛" (3 mm) at both ends with the hemostats. This will prevent the wires from poking through the hand fabric. Insert the chenille stems into the hands with hemostats. Stuff the tops of the fingers with the mini stuffing fork (see page 29).

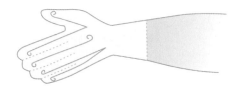

⑨ Stuff the hand and arm up to the elbow. Cut a chenille stem in half and crimp back the edges. Fold it in half again and twist it. Insert the stem into the doll arm so it is halfway above and below the elbow. Repeat with the remaining hand and arm.

⑩ Knot a double length of thread and wrap it around the elbows as you did the knees. This will secure the chenille stems and form a simple elbow detail that allows you to bend and pose the arms as desired.

⑪ Stuff the upper arms, leaving a 1" (2.5 cm) gap at the top. Close and gather the top edges of the arm openings with a long running stitch. Leave the raw edges exposed and knot the thread. Set the arms aside.

Making the Bodice and Attaching the Arms

① Cut a strip of skirt fabric to 3½"× 8" (8.9 × 20.3 cm) for the bodice.

② Fold the fabric in half, right sides together, and sew a center back seam with a ¼" (6 mm) seam allowance.

③ Press the top edge of the bodice ½" (1.3 cm) to the inside. Put the upper dress on the doll and pin it in place so the seam is in the center back. Tack the top edge into place at each shoulder.

④ In front, fold a vertical pleat on each side of the center to fit the bodice at the waist. Tack the pleats at the bottom edge to hold them together.

⑤ Hand-sew the arms to the torso at the shoulders securely with heavy nylon thread.

Making the Head

If you will be using the full-color face transfer, the facial features will be done before you construct the head. If you are creating your own facial features on your doll, the head will be constructed first, and then you will draw in the features. The pattern pieces for the head will have cutting and stitching lines indicated on them to guide you.

Using the Full-Color Face Transfer:

① To use the full-color face transfer, copy the transfer from page 112 onto a printer fabric sheet using an ink-jet printer, not a toner-based printer. Heat set the transfer according to the manufacturer's instructions. Once the transfer has been heat set, trace the outer guide lines with a purple fade-away marker, letting the ink bleed through to the other side.

② Fold the facial features down the center with the right sides together, matching the purple traced outer edges of the guideline. Place the head front pattern template on the fabric, lining up the outer traced edges with the pattern edges. Trace the chin and forehead darts lightly with a mechanical pencil. Skip to step 3 to construct the head.

Drawing Your Own Face:

① Fold a piece of plain, ivory fabric on the straight grain.

② Lay the head front pattern piece along the fold line, and trace around it lightly with a mechanical pencil, including the chin and forehead. Continue to step 3 to construct the head.

③ Stitch the forehead and chin seams into a dartlike shape. Be sure to stitch the chin smoothly to a full curve so the doll doesn't have a pointed chin.

④ Cut the head front directly on the solid, marked cutting line, but leave a ¼" (6 mm) seam allowance at the chin and forehead seams.

⑤ Place the head back pattern template on the head fabric that is folded with right sides together, and trace it with a mechanical pencil. Stitch the head back on the dotted stitching line as shown in the illustration at left.

⑥ Cut the head back directly on the solid, marked cutting line, but leave a ¼" (6 mm) seam allowance at the stitched seam.

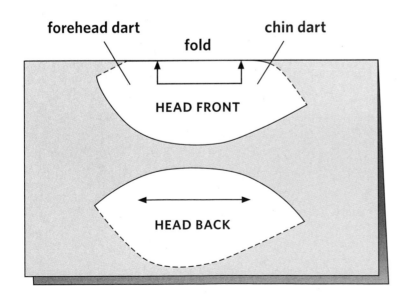

forehead dart   chin dart

fold

HEAD FRONT

HEAD BACK

⑦ Pin the head front to the head back with several pins, right sides and tops together. Sew a generous ⅛" (3 mm) seam all around the head. Sew carefully and catch all the edges.

⑧ Slash through the head back with sharp scissors as indicated on the back template. Turn the head right side out and stuff it firmly.

Creating the Facial Features on the Plain Fabric Face

It is a good idea to make several heads so you can enjoy learning how to color and shade the faces. Remember it is the *process* that is fun, so enjoy your learning curve! Experiment with different looks, colors, feature sizes, and expressions on your practice faces. Look through fashion magazines, art books, portrait photography, and at your own face for inspiration.

Most people find that there is one side of the face that is easier to draw than the other. When you begin to draw the features, work on the more difficult side first, and then follow with the easy side. This is something I learned years ago when making porcelain doll faces. If you do your best work on the easy side, it will be hard to match the work on your hard side. It is helpful to turn the head upside down as you work on the side that is harder for you. Keeping the features even and similar in size will create a balanced face.

Refer to my illustration of the transfer face for size and coloration. View the illustrations and photo images for feature placement and refer to the disappearing ink lines that are explained here; they are a great help. A purple fade-away marking pen works best.

Preparing the Face

① Draw a line down the center of the face from the forehead dart to the chin dart with a purple fade-away pen and the slide hem gauge.

② Draw a second line across the face from ear to ear to divide the face into quarters. Use the same marker and hem gauge.

③ Draw two more lines from the top to the bottom, ½" (1.3 cm) from the centerline, as shown. Draw one more line from side to side, ¼" (6 mm) above the centerline.

Drawing the Eyes

① Draw a circle with the brown Pigma pen to create each iris. See the illustration below for placement.

② Draw an oval around each iris with the black Pigma pen.

③ Color in the iris with a light blue gel pen or colored pencil.

④ Outline the iris with a blue, green, or brown Pigma pen to define the iris and add color depth.

⑤ Draw in the pupil with a black Pigma pen, letting the pupil circle touch the top edge of the oval. Enhance the top eye line again with black Pigma pen.

(6) Color the corners of each eye with a white gel pen. Repeat two or three times for good color saturation. Let the ink dry between coats.

(7) Highlight each iris at two o'clock with a white gel pen or white acrylic paint.

(8) Draw a crease line just over the top of each eye with a brown Pigma pen. Notice the line does not extend all the way to the corners.

(9) Add upper lashes with a black Pigma pen so they swing off the top eye line beyond the brown crease line. Notice the direction of the lashes is different on the left and right eyes. Add the bottom lashes.

Drawing the Nose and Mouth

(1) Measure approximately ¼" (6 mm) down from the center line and draw a small line with a fade-away fabric pen. Measure approximately ½" (1.3 cm) below the center line and use the same pen to draw another line marking the division of the top and bottom lips.

(2) Draw the nose detail as shown with the brown Pigma pen.

(3) Draw a lazy M and a lazy U to create the mouth with the brown Pigma pen. Color in the top lip with a dark rose colored pencil. Color the lower lip lighter than the top lip and highlight with a white gel pen.

(4) Deepen the color of the nostril holes with a dark gray colored pencil.

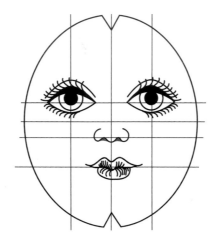

Drawing the Eyebrows and Shading the Face

I like to use powdered eye shadows and blushes to color in the facial features. They blend well and are readily available in attractive colors. Combine three eye shadow colors to add depth and life to the eyes. Don't be afraid to add lots of color.

(1) Dot the eyebrow in an arch shape with the purple fade-away marker to give you a preview of how the brow will look, so you can change the shape or placement if you aren't happy with it. Once you are happy with the arch and the placement of the brow dots, ink them in with Pigma pen—either black or brown, or a combination.

(2) Blush the cheeks with a rosy pink blush powder and a sponge applicator. Use a circular scrubbing motion to blend the color.

(3) Dab a bit of blush on the tip of the nose. Avoid getting color near the flare of the nostrils.

(4) Apply darker eye shadow—midnight blue, dark brown, or mauve—from the eye crease line to the top eye line with the short liner brush. Apply a second color, lime green or golden yellow, just below the brows using the short liner brush. Apply a final teal or lavender eye shadow between the brow and the eye crease line.

(5) Add highlights at the side of the bridge of the nose and up to the brow with a darker eye shadow color such as gray, dark brown, or deep gold with the short liner brush.

(6) Take the finished face outside and spray it with a finish coat of fixative to set and hold the color. Let it dry.

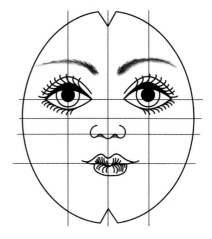

Attaching the Head

① Poke your finger up into the head opening to create a channel for the neck stem.

② Clamp the hemostats to the doll's neck and insert the neck into the head. Release and remove the hemostats. Move and position the head until you like the look. Poke the doll needle through the head and neck to hold the head in place.

③ Turn the raw edges of the head opening to the inside. Stitch the head onto the neck securely using a ladder stitch page 26. Stitch all around the head at least twice. Pull out the doll needle.

Making the Pantalets and Skirt

① Fold the pantalets fabric in half, right sides together, and place the fold line of the pantalets pattern on the fold of the fabric. Trace the pattern twice. Cut along all the lines except the fold line.

② Open flat the two pieces of fabric and pin them, right sides together, at the crotch seams. Stitch.

③ Pin the inseams together, aligning the crotch seams, and stitch the leg seam. Turn the pantalets right side out.

④ Hand-sew a running stitch with heavy nylon thread ½" (1.3 cm) from the top waist edge, leaving long tails of thread and no knots. Repeat ½" (1.3 cm) up from the bottom of each pant leg.

⑤ Slide the pantalets onto the doll and pull the waist threads to gather the pantalets to her snugly, tucking the top raw edges to the inside. Knot the threads in the back. Thread the tails back on a large needle and insert it into the doll's waist. Bring the needle out the front of the doll and snip the thread tails to bury them within the doll.

⑥ Pull the leg threads to gather each knee, folding the raw edges to the inside as they gather. Knot the thread tightly and bury the thread tails.

⑦ Tie lengths of ribbon into bows at each knee, if desired.

Making the Skirt

① Cut a piece of skirt fabric to 11" × 44" (27.9 × 111.8 cm). Fold it in half, right sides together, and sew a center back seam with a ¼" (6 mm) seam allowance.

② Fold one long edge under ¼" (6 mm) and then ½" (1.3 cm); press. Hand-sew or machine-stitch to hem. Hand- or machine-sew trim, lace, or ruffles to the hemmed edge as desired.

③ Trim loose threads and neaten the raw waist edge. Hand-sew a running stitch near the top edge with heavy nylon thread. Leave long thread tails and no knots.

④ Pull the skirt onto the doll. Pull the thread to gather the skirt to her waist and knot off the threads tightly in the back. Bury the thread tails. Leave the raw edges exposed on the skirt waist, as they will be covered by trim or ribbon later. Trim the edges free of loose threads.

Making the Optional Overskirt or Apron

This layer is optional, but I like the added texture and visual interest it creates. You can make a full skirt or just an apron, depending on the lace you have to work with. You can use an old handkerchief, a tea towel, ecru bridal lace, or some other vintage find.

① Cut a piece of lace to approximately 8" × 20" (20.3 × 50.8 cm).

② Hand-sew a running stitch along the top edge with heavy nylon thread. Leave long thread tails and no knots.

③ Pull the lace skirt over the top of the fabric skirt and pull the threads to gather it to her waist. Knot the threads securely in the back and bury them. If you are using a tea towel, turn under the raw edge at the waist as you gather it to the doll.

Making Optional Side Flounces

True to my motto, "More is better," I added side flounces to Jolie's costume, using two different silks. The dark brown is the same as the torso fabric, and the outer layer is a luxurious French knotted aqua silk. Dupioni silk is an excellent choice of fabric for decorative layers. Do not iron the silk after it has been sewn; it hangs much nicer if it's only finger-pressed.

① Layer the two silk fabrics, right sides together, and trace the flounce pattern onto the top layer. Stitch directly on the marked line, stopping as indicated. Cut around the stitching, leaving a generous seam allowance. Repeat for the second flounce.

② Carefully clip into the V indent of each scallop once.

③ Turn the flounces right side out and finger-press the scallops to shape them.

④ Hand-sew a running stitch with heavy nylon thread along the top of each flounce. Leave long thread tails and no knots.

⑤ Pull the threads to gather each flounce and to tie them around her waist. Adjust the gathers and the position of the flounces. Then, knot the threads and bury the thread tails.

⑥ Finger press the front edge of each flounce toward the back to create a lapel. Sew decorative buttons or charms to hold the lapel back.

Making the Sleeves

I made two layers for the sleeves—a silk puff at the shoulders and a narrow lace oversleeve. One layer is fine, but I like the two together over the upper arm fabric.

Lace Sleeves

① Cut 2 pieces of sheer lace to approximately 3" × 3" (7.6 × 7.6 cm). Fold each piece in half, right sides together, and stitch the edges together with a ¼" (6 mm) seam. Turn each sleeve right-side out.

② Pull the lace sleeves up onto the arms. Tack the sleeve directly to the arm to secure the top edge. Fold a small, vertical pleat in the top edge if necessary to fit it at the upper arm.

③ Tie a ribbon, cord, or narrow strip of tulle at the elbow, ½" (1.3 cm) above the bottom edge of the lace sleeve. This creates a small ruffled edge just below the elbow.

Puff Sleeves

① Cut 2 rectangles of silk to 4" × 10" (10.2 × 25.4 cm). Fold each piece in half, right sides together, and stitch the edges together with a ¼" (6 mm) seam. Turn the sleeves right side out.

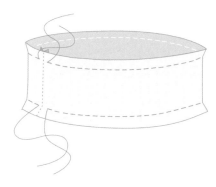

② Hand-sew a running stitch with heavy nylon thread along the top and bottom edges of each sleeve, leaving long thread tails and no knots.

③ Pull the sleeves onto the doll's arms, up to the shoulders. Pull the top threads, tucking the raw edges under as the fabric gathers. Pull the thread tight, knot the top edge, and bury the thread tails.

④ Pull the thread tails at the bottom edge of the sleeves, gathering and tucking under the raw edges. Knot off the thread securely and bury the thread tails.

> ### TIP
>
> When working with silk, only iron it before you sew. After you create your costume, don't iron the silk again. This will prevent the silk from flattening out at the seam edges, keeping your costume full and voluminous.

Making the Shoes

① Fold a piece of leather, suede, or Ultra-suede with right sides together. Trace the pattern twice, each time with the pattern fold line on the fabric fold.

② Stitch the top and heel of the shoe as shown. Leave the toe and the opening for the foot unstitched.

⑤ Turn the shoes right side out and pull them onto her feet.

⑥ Trace (on the wrong side) and cut two spats of leather or suede in a second color. Cut carefully, exactly on the lines.

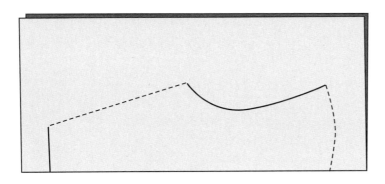

③ Cut out the shoes, leaving a small seam allowance along the stitching but cutting directly on the line at the top of the shoe opening and toe.

④ Stitch the toe and heel seams with right sides together as shown. Trim away excess fabric at the toe and heel.

⑦ Apply glue to the wrong side of the shoe spats and glue them directly over the feet and shoes.

⑧ Embellish the shoes as desired with bows, buckles, or buttons.

⑤ Scrunch the silk wrap down to create folds and pleats that conform to her head shape. Tack the folds at the center front, center back, and each side. Fold the pleats so the wrap fits the circumference of her head; stitch them down securely. Continue to tack down the scrunched pleats and folds.

⑥ Glue extra bits of hair fiber as needed under the head wrap.

⑦ Embellish the front of the head wrap as desired. I glued a velvet flower to the front of Jolie's head wrap.

Making the Hair and Head Wrap

① Glue bits of yarn hair or mohair all along the hairline. It isn't necessary to put hair over the entire head because it will be covered.

② Cut a piece of dupioni silk to 8" × 13–14" (20.3 × 33–35.6 cm). Stitch two sides as shown.

③ Turn the head wrap right side out and finger press the raw edge ½" (1.3 cm) to the inside.

④ Pull the square onto her head. Insert a straight pin through the wrap in the center front at her hairline and in the center back at the nape of her neck.

TIP

It is almost mandatory to use dupioni silk for the head wrap, as it scrunches up and contours into elegant folds.

Making the Trims

I often create my own embellishment trims from ribbons or rickrack. I used the following ribbon technique for the trim on Jolie's waist and each arm cuff.

① Start with 1½ (3.8 cm) yards of 1" (2.5 cm) soft ribbon. Cut 2 pieces, each 12" (30.5 cm) long, for each arm. Use the rest for the waist.

② Dab a thin line of glue at each raw edge and turn ⅛" (3 mm) to the wrong side.

③ Hand-sew a running stitch with heavy nylon thread as shown. Leave long thread tails and no knots.

④ Pull the thread to gather and scallop the ribbon. Wrap the short pieces around each arm to create a cuff and the long piece around the waist. Knot the threads to secure the ribbon and bury the thread tails. Stitch or glue into place for added security.

⑤ Glue or tack velvet ribbon or trim around the seam where the upper arm and hand fabrics meet.

Adding Finishing Touches

Shoe Embellishments

It's easy to make lovely simple rosettes for shoe embellishments or costume trim.

Take small lengths of rickrack, lace, ruffled trims, or pretty ribbons and sew a running stitch along one edge with heavy thread.

Pull the thread to gather, and knot off securely. As you pull the threads, the trims will gather up in to a lovely rosette. Add beads, buttons, sequins, or small charms to finish off as desired.

Lace Collar

Cut a piece of fine lace to ½" × 8" (1.3 × 20.3 cm) and hand-sew a running stitch along the top edge. Gather the thread and tie the lace around her neck. Knot off the threads and bury the tails.

TIP

Try tea-dyeing ribbons and trims for a vintage look. Put 10 to 15 tea bags and 1 teaspoon (6 g) salt into a large pan of boiling water. Let the tea bags steep for several minutes. Remove them and immerse your textiles. Let them soak for 1 hour or longer, depending on the depth of color you want. Rinse and dry the articles.

Waist and Torso Trim

Tie ribbon or trim at the waist to cover all the layers of nylon threads and any raw fabric edges. Glue trim pieces to the upper torso from the neck to the dress top.

Gallery

Tulla
by Val Zeitler

Mimes, clowns, and old boudoir dolls from the 1930s and '40s have always fascinated me. So this is my inspiration, and this is where I begin this journey.

My costume consists of a really pretty black dotted Swiss vintage-style fabric for the overdress. The overskirt is a muted silk velvet, and it has two tulle underskirts. A girl can never have too many underskirts, can she? So feminine!

I used colors reminiscent of the period I chose—all muted tones, nothing bright. I love to dye fabric and trims to suit the mood, so I hand-dyed the fabric for the hat, ribbon trim, corset, and legs. Ball fringe is another favorite of mine. It adds a bit of funk and whimsy at the same time. I used a rich black felt for the doll's pointed collar and her lace-up boots.

I normally start by working on a doll's face, but for some reason I started dressing this one first and then, when she was all dressed, I did her face. I added sculpted eyelids to give depth to her face and to achieve the look I was striving for—a sort of mime or clown with a bit of boudoir doll appearance. I like the dreamy, whimsical look she has.

I really enjoyed working on this doll. It was a lot of fun. I found everything I needed to create my doll right in my workroom; I bet you can too! Use your imagination and just go with it.

Elegant Jolie
by Christine Mary Howard

Generally, I prefer to use natural fabrics such as silk and linen. For Elegant Jolie, I used a tightly woven pima cotton for the face, hands, and feet. I chose a silk for the torso. The skirt is randomly dyed silk velvet with a petticoat of silk chiffon. I used a candle to singe the hemline of each. I love the drape of silk for dolls, and it is so easy to dye for a special effect.

For the hair, I used layers of lace and silk chiffon, and I used a soldering iron to give the hairdo a wild, tousled look. The elegant, jaunty pillbox hat is simply the lid from a purchased round beaded box. I used suede to make the peplum and shoes, and I embellished the collar and shoes with lovely antique buttons.

My personal challenge was, through the use of color only, to visually create depth and dimension on a flat face doll. It is amazing how much depth you can get with color on a flat face pattern.

I hadn't made many cloth dolls recently. However, Elegant Jolie was so easy to make and went together so perfectly that now I can't stop making her. I have made several more since the first!

Erin
by Colleen Babcock

I imagined my Erin dressed in Irish Renaissance fashion with the billowing sleeves of an Irish chemise, dancing as she played the Celtic drum, the bodhran (bow-rahn). And of course she needed a lace bodice to go with it.

I dampened a piece of parfait pink–colored Pimatex for the body and covered the surface with watered-down ocher Jacquard's Dyna Flow. The mix of the pink fabric and yellow dye gave me the perfect complexion for a redhead. After making up the body, I wanted to give a bit more curve to her figure, so I glued two pompoms to her chest. I also weighted her bottom with lead shot so she sits well.

I drew the face with a mix of colored and watercolor pencils, shading and highlighting to give the flat face the impression of shape. Once I tacked and glued her hair in place, the costume came together quickly. I particularly enjoyed making the tiny shoes out of dyed mulberry bark and the drum out of the inner circle of an embroidery hoop and some leather. As I went on, elements of Irish culture insinuated themselves into the details of the doll—the lace at the bottom of the bloomers, the writing on the fabric of the skirt lining, and the green and rolling land of Ireland itself in the crazy-quilted fabric of the cloak. This doll is wrapped in the warmth and music of the Irish.

Odessa
by Jill McCloy

I fantasized about Erté (the greatest costume designer of all time, in my opinion) while constructing the body and playing with the head, using some new-to-me and well-written techniques by Barbara. The body came together, and I opted for a simplified costume composed of a favorite Erté-inspired jacket and pants from Bali, plus a high scrunched neckline, sleeves, and a turban. With a bit of fiddling, the paper towel patterns were ready.

I chose Odessa's colors based on the availability of rayon fabric, needed for its drape. Odessa, once dressed and lightly embellished, was ready for her footwear. Her first boots, in red, made her look like a superhero in search of a cape, so I cut down the cuff and went with basic black and a tiny bit of beaded embellishment. It worked.

I'm not sure when the doll became Odessa. I hadn't been thinking of names, but that is her name and this is her story.

Elspeth
by Teresa Malyon

I wanted to create a flapper, but I wanted to push my limits and leave my comfort zone.

My flapper clothing is made from a sumptuous piece of wide Nottingham lace that had been squirreled away for many years awaiting the perfect doll. The torso and skirt are made of cream dupioni silk with an overlay of the same lace to give a fuller look without detracting too much from the sharp pleating of the skirt underneath.

The little skullcap, typical of the era, is made from another lace, which I heavily beaded around the edge. It hugs her head to expose the sharp lines of the hairstyle framing her pretty face.

Her shoes are made from the softest cream leather and are quite plain so they don't overwhelm her ensemble.

The stole is made from lengths of marabou feather, which are sewn on both sides and down the center of a piece of cream dupioni with tassels, the final touch, at each end.

Turkish Delight
by Donna Perry

Looking at the pattern pieces for Jolie, I could see that she was an elegant, ultrafeminine doll. I pieced the body pattern at the bustline using flesh-colored cotton fabric to create a décolletage for the burgundy silk empire bodice, and I used the green dupioni for the torso. I made her legs from green and metallic gold cotton. The heavy tapestry fabric became a short jacket with bell sleeves, which I made by drafting a pattern using a draped paper towel. The front edge is bound with a bias strip of gold metallic cotton and embellished with French green silk braid and gold ribbon. These fabrics are repeated in the skirt, along with amethyst and gold beading along the seam line and gold lace tacked to the underside. I took tiny darts at the skirt top to cut down bulk. Four gathered tubes of fabric became the sleeves.

Two bias strips of burgundy silk were wrapped and tacked to her feet to become ballet slippers. A bias burgundy silk scrap became a dropped-waist sash, complete with an antique button for accent. Scraps of yarn and needlework fibers were combined and sewn on for hair, and her face was defined using colored pencils and gel pens. A little lace, more beads, and a few bows here and there, and she was finished.

4 Creating Danielle

A Detailed Cloth Doll with a Soft-Sculpted Face

There are many ways to approach the art of soft sculpting. In this chapter, I am delighted to share my self-taught doll-sculpting experiences with you. The techniques used to create Danielle are more advanced that those used to make the other dolls presented in this book. Danielle is a seated doll. Her body parts were designed for a permanent seated pose, unlike Jolie, who is flexible at her joints.

Danielle has button-jointed hips and shoulders, wired hands, and a face created by soft-sculpting knit fabric.

Soft sculpting is a technique that takes time and practice to develop. Embrace the learning curve and experiment with several kinds of knit fabric. Keep in mind that we are processed-oriented here. It is the process that provides the challenge sense of accomplishment and ultimate joy.

Choosing the right fabrics for your doll will greatly affect your results. Knit fabric is essential for Danielle's face, and for successful soft sculpting of her face. I recommend a two-way stretch cotton Lycra blend; the Lycra offers memory, and the cotton fibers offer a nice matte finish.

The cotton fibers dye beautifully while the Lycra is resistant to color, so the blend offers soft, pleasing results. T-shirt and silk knits also work fine if that's your preference.

Look for knit fabrics with a smooth texture with no obvious slubs. You can dye white knit fabric ivory with a commercial dye to match ivory fabric for the torso and hands (page 76). Woven cotton fabrics in ivory are readily available.

Woven fabrics are used for the construction of Danielle's arms, legs, and torso. I often choose colorful cottons, silks, and even velvets for some parts of the body. Danielle's upper arms are made from a beautiful mauve dupioni silk and her torso

is moss-green silk velvet. Silk and velvet can be a bit fussy. Always allow extra seam allowance for dupioni silk. If you also choose to use silk velvet for the torso, iron on a fusible stabilizer to the backside of the fabric.

The gallery section is an inspiration as the doll makers unleashed their inner artist to delight us with their unique talents. Bravo!

Creating Danielle

MATERIALS

Many of the supplies you probably have on hand, but some are doll-specific and you'll want them at your fingertips before starting your project.

- 3–4 pieces heavy paper or card stock for template
- ⅓ yard (0.3 m) woven fabric for the legs (I used polka-dot cotton)
- ¼ yard (0.25 m) woven fabric for the upper arms (I used mauve dupioni silk)
- ¼ yard (0.25 m) woven fabric for the lower torso (I used moss-green silk velvet)
- ¼ yard (0.25 m) ivory woven cotton fabric for the hands and upper torso
- ¼ yard (0.25 m) ivory cotton Lycra knit (with two-way stretch) for the face
- ½ yard (0.5 m) silk organza for the side flounces (I used moss-green silk organza.)
- ⅓ yard (0.3 m) silk dupioni for the pantalets and upper puff sleeves, wrong side sleeve cuffs (I used lavender silk dupioni.)
- ¼ yard (0.25 m) silk dupioni for the sleeve cuffs and hat (I used raspberry dupioni.)
- ¼ yard (0.25 m) each of moss-green and bright green dupioni silk for the knee scallops
- cotton-wrapped polyester threads to match fabrics
- heavy nylon upholstery thread
- bag of fiberfill, such as Fairfield's Soft Touch Supreme
- white and light blue or green gel pens
- colored pencils, two lip colors and dark gray
- black, brown, and green Pigma pens, 005 or 01 tip, such as Sakura Micron Pigma Pens
- powdered, colored eye shadows and blushes
- flat ½" (1.3 cm), stiff brush for blending powders
- spray art fixative, such as Krylon
- tacky glue
- clear fabric glue, such as Fabri Tac
- 2 chenille stems

- 2 ⅝" (1.6 cm) buttons for shoulder jointing
- Two 1¼" (3.2 cm) buttons for hip jointing
- tan and yellow fabric dye, such as Rit or Dylon (optional)
- hair fibers
- small black glass beads for eyes
- ribbons, trims, laces, beads, buttons, pompoms, baubles, and charms
- small pieces of thin leather or Ultrasuede in 2 or 3 colors for the shoes
- small piece of heavy leather for the soles (old belts work well here)
- small piece of poster board for inner sole material

TOOLS

- sewing machine
- open-toe appliqué foot
- straight pins
- sharp scissors
- makeup sponge wand applicators
- short liner brush
- measuring tape
- disappearing ink fabric marker (purple fade-away)
- mechanical lead pencil
- 6" (15.2 cm) metal hem gauge with slide indicator
- straight-nose hemostats
- stuffing forks, regular and mini
- ⅛" (3 mm) brass turning tube and rod
- long darners #7, such as John James, for soft sculpting the face
- 5" or 7" (12.7 or 17.8 cm) doll needle
- steam iron
- spritz bottle with water
- hand sewing needle
- emery board
- screw punch

Dyeing Knit Fabric

As previously discussed, you might want to dye your knit fabric to get a precise color. I like working with Rit dye, which is widely available in the United States and Australia, and Dylon dye, which is available in the United Kingdom.

Refer to the dyeing instructions on the dye package, keeping in mind that results will vary depending on the amount of fabric you are dyeing, its fiber content, the temperature of the water, and the length of time you leave the fabric immersed in the dye bath.

The following instructions are for dyeing fabric in a washing machine with a combination of yellow and tan Rit dye powders to create an ivory color.

1. Prewash, rinse, and spin the knit fabric in your washing machine. Remove the damp fabric and set it aside. Do not dry it.

2. Set your washing machine for hot water and a small-size load.

3. Add ½ teaspoon (2 g) tan powder dye and ½ (2 g) teaspoon yellow powder dye to the water. Agitate the water to mix the dyes.

4. Test the color by dipping a small strip of fabric into the dye bath. For a darker color, add more dye. For a lighter color, add more water.

5. Immerse the damp knit fabric in the dye bath and leave it in until it is the desired color. Once the fabric is the perfect shade, remove it from the washing machine and set it aside.

6. Spin the colored water out of the washing machine and refill it with hot water.

7. Immerse the dyed fabric in the hot water and set the washing machine to spin to remove all the excess water.

8. Dry the fabric in the clothes dryer at a hot setting.

Determining Straight Grain and Fabric Front

Knit fabric has a distinct straight grain. It is important to lay out the pattern piece so the arrow on the pattern aligns with the straight grain of the fabric.

Cutting the doll's head on the straight grain affects the development and shape of the soft sculpting. Be sure to correctly identify the straight grain and the right and wrong sides of the fabric. Once you have identified the straight grain, you can easily identify the right or skin side for the doll.

When you stretch the fabric in one direction, one side will have defined ribs and the other a more meshlike appearance. The ribbed side is the straight grain, and the mesh is the skin side. When you stretch the fabric in the opposite direction, the ribs blur and the result is the cross-grain. If you are unsure about the straight grain, ask for clarification at your fabric store or examine a knit shirt. On knit garments, the rib side is the outer side of the garment and the straight grain runs from top to bottom.

Getting Started

Read through the project instructions to get a good overview of the steps before starting the doll. This will help you visualize what lies ahead and collect your materials in advance.

Prepare all the pattern templates for Danielle (page 119–125). Refer to the instructions for template-method sewing (page 25). The patterns include torso, leg, head, arm, pantalets, knee scallop, sleeve cuff, hat brim, shoe upper, shoe sole, shoe topper, and shoe sling strap.

Creating the Torso

① With right sides together and a ¼" (6 mm) seam allowance, sew the chosen torso fabric to the ivory-colored fabric. Fold the seamed fabric, right sides together, and position the torso pattern template on it so the marking on the pattern aligns with the seam, as shown. Trace the template with the fade-away fabric marker (**A**).

② Set the sewing machine for a 1.5 stitch length and sew directly on the traced line, except for the top of the neck. Cut out the torso, leaving a generous ¼" (6 mm) seam allowance all around. Do not clip any curves. Dab tacky glue with your fingertip to the raw neck edges to protect the fabric from fraying.

③ When the glue is dry, turn the torso right side out with the hemostats. Stuff the torso firmly, using the hemostats and stuffing fork to insert the fiberfill. Whipstitch the neck opening closed. The torso must be full and firm, but not rock-hard. The neck should be firm and stable.

④ Glue trim around the upper torso to cover the seam where the two fabrics meet, overlapping the ends at the side seam, under the arm, so they are not highly visible. Glue trim down the center front of the torso, as desired. Set the torso aside.

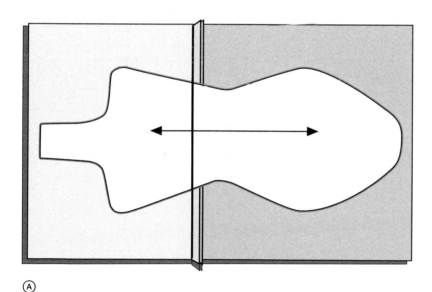

Ⓐ

TIP

I always steam-iron the neck after I stuff it. Spritz with a fine mist of water or spray starch and press the neck on each side. Do not flatten it, but apply light pressure and let the steam do the magic. I often steam the arms and legs as well, after they have been stuffed, to smooth the texture of the stuffing beneath the fabric skin.

Creating the Legs

1. Fold the leg fabric in half, right sides together. Position the leg pattern template so the straight-grain arrow is on the straight grain of the fabric and trace it twice, leaving at least 1" (2.5 cm) of space between the legs.

2. Stitch both legs directly on the traced line, leaving the tops of the legs un-stitched. Cut out the legs, leaving a generous ¼" (6 mm) seam allowance around the seams. Clip once behind each knee.

3. Turn the legs right side out. Hand-sew the running stitch with heavy nylon upholstery thread around the top of each leg as shown. Leave long tails of thread to tie off later (**B**).

4. Stuff the legs firmly, especially the ankles (page 28). Pull the threads at the top of the legs to gather and close the top. Knot the threads securely and bury the tails of the thread in the legs. Don't turn under the top raw edges because they will be covered by the pantalets.

5. Hand- or machine-stitch across the top of each foot at the toes to flatten them for the shoes that come later (**C**).

Creating the Arms and Hands

1. Pin the upper arm and hand fabrics, with right sides together. Stitch with ¼" (6 mm) seam allowance. Press the seam allowances toward the upper arm fabric. Apply a thin line of tacky glue to hold down the seam allowances.

2. Fold the seamed fabric, right sides together. Position the arm pattern template so the straight-grain arrow is on the straight grain of the fabric and the pattern marking is directly over the fabric seam (**D**).

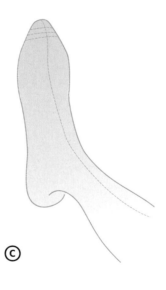

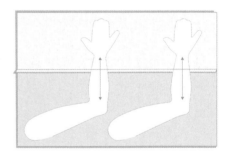

Ⓑ

Ⓓ

③ Trace the arm pattern twice, leaving at least 2" (5.1 cm) between the two arms. There is no need to flip the pattern piece to create a right and left arm. Use the mechanical pencil to lightly trace around the hand. Use a white gel pen to trace the upper arm if you can't see the pencil lines. Make secondary marks on the hands with the purple fade-away pen as shown to widen the space between the fingers, making more room for stitching (**E**).

E

④ Stitch the lower arm and hands along the new markings with ivory-colored thread. As you approach the V between the thumb and the mitt, take 2 stitches straight across. Repeat between the fourth and fifth fingers (**F**).

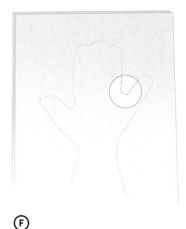

F

⑤ Stitch the upper arms with matching thread, leaving an opening near the top of each arm as indicated on the pattern. Cut the arms and hands around the stitching, leaving a gen-erous ¼" (6 mm) seam allowance around the stitching and a ¾" (1.9 cm) seam allowance at the opening. The extra fabric at the opening will protect the seam allowance when you turn the arms right side out and stuff them.

6. Trim the seam allowance slightly narrower around the hand. Clip right up to the stitching between the thumb and mitt and the fourth and fifth fingers. Clip once on the inside of each elbow.

7. Insert the brass tube inside the arm into the thumb. From the outside, use the rod to press the tip of the thumb firmly against the tube opening. Roll the thumb up onto the rod to help turn it right side out. Repeat for the little finger. Insert the hemostats into the hand and pull the mitt and arm right side out. Poke the thumb and little finger all the way out (**G**).

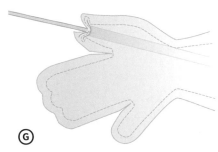

G

8. Referring to the pattern, draw finger details with the purple fade-away marker on the mitt section of the hand as shown. Hand- or machine-stitch the finger details. I much prefer to do this by hand with a single knotted thread. Bury all the thread tails in the hand (**H**).

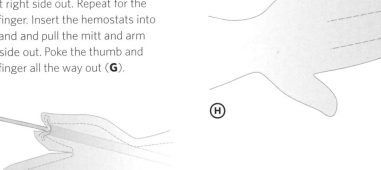

H

9. Cut chenille stems to wire the fingers. Crimp back ⅛" (3 mm) at each end with the hemostats. This prevents the wires from poking through the hand fabric. Insert the chenille stems into the hands with the hemostats. Stuff the tops of the fingers with the mini stuffing fork (page 29) (**I**).

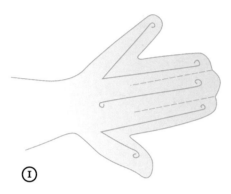

(**I**)

10. Stuff the top and palm side of each hand, using the hemostats to sandwich stuffing between the wires. Continue to firmly stuff the hands. Then stuff the wrists and arms, using the regular stuffing fork or the hemostats. Make the wrist especially firm.

11. Stuff all the way to the top of the arms and whipstitch the openings closed.

12. For the sleeve cuffs, pin two pieces of silk, each a different color, right sides together (I used raspberry on the outside and lavender on the inside). Trace two sleeve cuffs onto the fabrics. Sew on the traced line, leaving the stitching open as indicated on the pattern.

13. Cut around the stitching with a generous ¼" (6 mm) seam allowance. Clip up to the stitching between each scallop. Turn the cuffs right side out and finger-press the scallops smooth. Do not iron the cuff if you are using silk fabric, as the iron will flatten the silk.

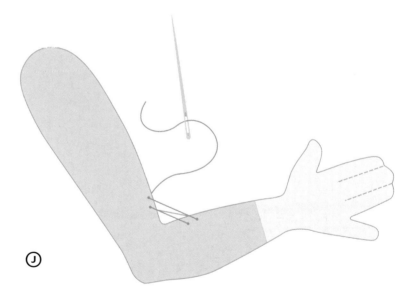

(**J**)

14. Whipstitch the top opening of each cuff closed. Sew beads as desired along the length of the cuff to look like buttons.

15. Wrap a cuff around each upper arm and whipstitch the ends together to fit the arms snugly. Glue or sew trim around the upper wrist to conceal the seam that joins the arm and hand.

16. If you like, bend one of the arms up and stitch it in place with small hand-stitches on the inside elbow. This gives the doll a varied pose without having to use different arm pattern pieces (**J**).

String-Jointing the Arms and Legs

Refer to the illustration below for arm and leg positioning. Work with a double length of heavy nylon upholstery thread and a doll needle (**K**).

① Position the arms at the shoulders with a flat button on the outside of each arm. Run the thread through one button, the arm, the torso, the opposite arm, and the other button, leaving a long thread tail at the first button. Insert the needle back through the button and bring it back through the arm, torso, arm, and opposite button. Tie the threads into a secure, tight knot. Dab glue on the knot and bury the thread tails back in the doll. The knot should be so tight that the doll holds her own pose.

② Repeat step 1 to joint the legs. The doll should be able to hold herself upright and not fall forward.

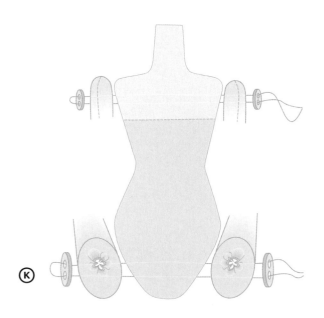

(K)

Making the Head

I suggest you make at least two or three heads so you can practice stuffing the head and sculpting the face.

① Identify the right and wrong side of the two-way stretch knit fabric and the straight grain, as described earlier (page 76). Lay the face template on the right side of the fabric with the straight-grain arrow on the straight grain of the fabric. Trace around it once with the fade-away marker and cut it out directly on the traced line.

② Make all the markings and lines with the purple fade-away marker. Draw a straight line down the center of the face from the forehead to the chin on the skin side of the knit fabric. Sew a running stitch with heavy nylon upholstery thread around the edge of the face, beginning and ending at the marked line. Leave long thread tails and no knots (**L**).

③ Pull the threads to gather the fabric into a pouch with the purple line on the outside. Hold the threads in one hand and use your thumbs to shove medium wads of stuffing in the pouch. Fill the pouch as much as possible without completely stretching the fabric. It should be full but not hard or too firm. The head should measure from top to bottom (forehead to chin) about 2¼" (5.8 cm); if it is bigger, remove some of the stuffing.

④ Pull the threads tight and knot them off in the back of the head, closing the opening completely. Trim the thread tails to 3–4" (7.6–10.2 cm) long and leave them out in the back. Dab the knot with tacky glue.

⑤ Distribute the fiberfill inside the head to form a nice oval or egg shape. Do this by piercing the fabric with the tip of the needle toward the inner surface of the knit fabric. Make sure the edges of the oval are smooth and even.

> **TIP**
>
> Remember to make all your markings with a purple fade-away marker, not a water-soluble marker.

Ⓛ

General Sculpting Guidelines

- One oval of fabric will make one head.

- Sculpting is done with side-to-side stitches not back-to-front or top-to-bottom stitches, unless otherwise directed.

- Do not stitch diagonally through the head, unless directed to do so, as cross-tension will distort the shape of the head and face.

- The thread and most of the stitches will lie beneath the fabric, inside the head and not on the surface of the face, unless otherwise directed.

- Change the thread on the needle frequently so it doesn't break. Work with cotton-wrapped polyester or 100 percent polyester thread and a sculpting needle.

- Work with a single thread throughout the entire sculpting process.

- Take care not to push the fabric down or compress it with your fingers during stitching. This could embed the needle and thread deep in the stuffing, which would distort the facial features.

- Use the top of the needle like a digging tool when directed, to move and manipulate the stuffing forward. Dig and pull the stuffing toward the surface of the face to create a small mound of compacted stuffing for the nose, nostril flares, cheeks, lips, and chin when directed. If you dig too deep, the mound will appear swollen; if you go too shallow, there will be no dimension.

- Practice sculpting on those multiple heads you made earlier!

Sculpting the Face

To sculpt the face, use regular-weight cotton-wrapped polyester thread and a sculpting needle. I recommend the John James brand #7 long darning needle. It's flexible and long enough to pass through the doll head, but it won't make holes in the fabric. Change the thread often, because it tends to wear and fatigue as it passes through the fabric so many times. Work with a single length of knotted thread; a double thread will make bigger holes in the fabric.

Preparing the Face and Head

① Draw a line across the face from ear to ear with the fade-away marker, to quarter the face. Refer to the illustration and mark the placement dots and circle on the face (**M**).

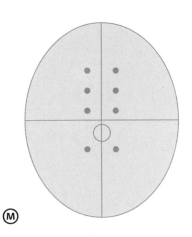

Ⓜ

② In the Sculpting Guide Illustration, notice the dots are numbered. The dots represent the needle insertion locations. Dots 6 and 8 are the same hole as are dots 5, 9, and 11. This numbering makes it easier to follow a stitching sequence (**N**).

Sculpting Guide

2 ●   ● 1

4 ●   ● 3

8, 6 ●   ● 5, 9, 11

◯

7 ●   ● 10

Ⓝ

Note: #6 and #8 are the same hole as are # 5, 9 and 11. This is numbered so we can followed in numerical sequence.

Nose Sculpting, Photo Guide 1

Use the tip of the needle to dig and move a small mound of stuffing forward to create a bump just beneath the marked circle, this will be the fullest part of the nose.

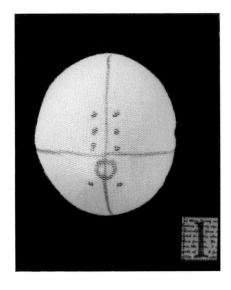

Nose Sculpting, Photo Guide 2

- Anchor the thread with two or three straight stitches in the back of the head near the closed hole.

- Insert the needle in the back of the head and bring it out the front of the head at marking #1.

- Reinsert the needle at marking #1, one or two threads of fabric away from the exit hole. Scoop a bit of stuffing so it is under the needle and exit at marking #2. The deeper you scoop, the broader the bridge of the nose will be.

- Re-enter at marking #2, scoop, and exit at marking #3.

- Re-enter at marking #3, scoop, and exit at marking #4.

- Re-enter at marking #4, scoop, and exit at marking #5.

- Re-enter at marking #5, scoop, and exit at marking #6.

- Pull the stitches taut to form the beginnings of a nose bridge. Dig beneath the circle again with the tip of the needle to retrain the nose bump.

- Re-enter at marking #6, bring the needle straight down, and exit at marking #7.

- Re-enter at marking #7 and bring the needle straight back up to exit at marking #8.

- Repeat the last two steps, stitching from marking #6 to #7 and back to #8 to hold the thread tension.

- Re-enter at marking #8 and exit at marking #9.

- Re-enter at marking #9 and bring the needle straight down and exit at marking #10.

- Re-enter at marking #10 and exit at marking #11.

- Repeat the last two steps, stitching from marking #9 to #10 and back to #11 to hold the thread tension.

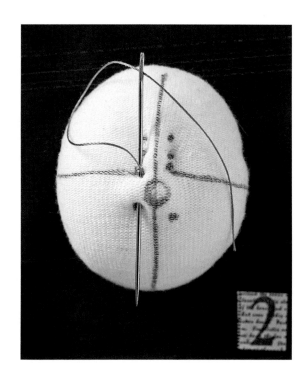

This section of stitching is numerically out of order, but it will permanently anchor the stuffing into the nose bump.

- Pierce the fabric with the tip of the needle and pull the stuffing forward behind the nose circle to fill it out completely. This will be the final shape of the nose.

- Insert the needle in marking #11 and out at marking #7.

- Re-enter at marking #7 and exit at marking #11.

- Re-enter at marking #11 and exit at marking #8.

- Re-enter at marking #8 and exit at marking #10.

- Re-enter at marking #10 and exit at marking #8. Re-enter at marking #8 and exit at marking #5.

- If any of the stitches slipped or seem incorrect, re-enter through any marking and restitch to correct the tension and shape of the nose.

- To change the thread, bring the needle through to the back of the head and knot off the thread behind one of the eyes without pulling or creating tension on the thread. Start a new single, knotted thread by anchoring a few stitches on the back of the head. Bring the needle out at marking #5 (**O**).

- Follow the stitching illustration to the right for stitch placement between the previous stitching to narrow and finish the bridge of the nose. Anchor the tension, re-enter at marking #5, and exit at marking #6.

- From marking #6, follow the grey dots in the illustration below, and stitch in between the original stitches that form the bridge of the nose (6–1), ending at marking 1.

- Bring the needle to the back of the head and anchor off the tension.

- Bring the needle through the head at #6.

- Re-enter at #6 and come out at #5.

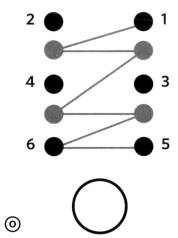

Sculpting Guide

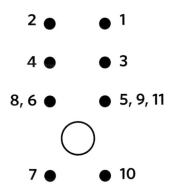

2 ●   ● 1

4 ●   ● 3

8, 6 ●   ● 5, 9, 11

7 ●   ● 10

Nostrils Sculpting, Photo Guide 3

Create the nostril flares by using the tip of your needle like a tool to scrape small bits of stuffing to each side of the nose. Insert the needle tip into the nostrils and scrape small wads of stuffing from the cheek area. These bits of stuffing should be the same size on each side, and you should be able to feel the bump beneath the fabric.

• Insert four straight pins at an angle beyond the desired location for the nostril flares, as shown. This is an exaggerated placement, as the stitches will pull the nostril flares smaller than your pin placement. *Note: This is the first time the thread will lie on the outside of the fabric. The threads need to be pulled very tight to hold the wads of stuffing in place and complete the nostril flare. If at any*

time the nostril flare loops become loose, just clip the threads and re-stitch. These stitches often have to be done more than once to get them to hold firm. Also note that if the nostril flares are not even or the same fullness, clip the thread on one side, re-establish the bump and place the anchor pins. Stitch as before to secure the flare.

• Follow illustration **P**. Pick up your needle at marking #5 and follow the illustration to position the thread behind the pins and enter marking #10. Come straight up to marking #5.

• Re-enter marking #5 and go straight down and exit marking #10.

• Re-enter marking #10 and then back up one more time at #5 to hold the thread tension taut and to create the nostril flare.

• Reenter at marking #5 and cross under the fabric to exit at marking #6.

• Wrap the thread around the second set of pins from marking #6 to the nostril hole at marking #7.

• Enter marking #7 and stitch straight up to exit at marking #6.

• To hold the tension of the nostril flare threads, re-enter at marking #6 and exit at marking #7.

• Re-enter at marking #7 and stitch straight up to exit at #6.

• Remove the pins. The threads should hold the nostril flare.

• Use the tip of the needle to shape and pull out the tip of the nose by piercing the fabric and tugging it forward.

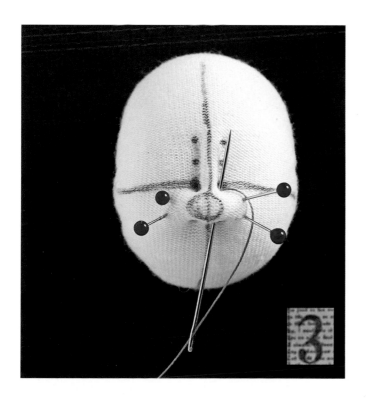

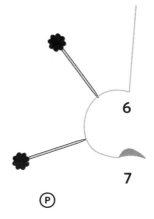

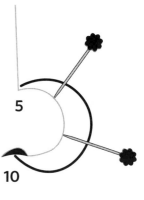

P

Eye Sculpting

This is an excellent time to change thread again. Take the thread from the front nostril area directly to the back of the head and knot off. Secure the thread behind one of the eyes. Do not pull any tension from the front of the face to the back of the head.

- Mark two eye dots with the fade-away marker so they are level with the top of the bridge of the nose.

- Select two small black or dark colored beads for the eyes that are the same size. Make sure your needle will pass through the bead holes.

- Anchor your new single, knotted thread in the back of the head and come out through the front of the face at one of the eye dots. Go through the bead, and re-enter on the opposite side of the eye dot and go back through the head, pulling tension on the thread to indent the bead. Anchor the tension and knot off the thread in the back of the head directly behind that eye. *Note: This entry and exit will tie the bead on so the hole runs horizontally and not vertically. This will give more light reflection in the eyes.*

- Take a large stitch across the back of the head and anchor it at the back of the head behind the second eye. Repeat the process that you did for the first eye to stitch on the second eye bead.

- Check that the tension (indent) is the same for each eye. Re-stitch one or both until they are the same. As you work on each side of the face, stitch directly behind that particular eye area; do not create diagonal stitching across the head from one eye to the other.

TIP

If your needle doesn't fit through the bead, try this: After you bring the needle through the fabric, take the thread off the needle. Take the thread through the bead without the needle and then put the thread back on the needle and continue stitching the head as directed.

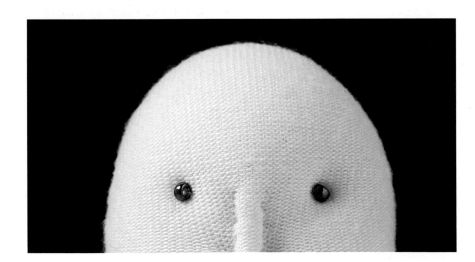

Upper Lip Sculpting, Photo Guide 4

- Measure with the hem gauge and draw a horizontal line with the fade-away marker a generous ¼" (6 mm) down from and directly under the nose. This line represents the middle of the mouth.

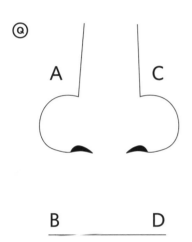

- Make two dots with a fade-away marker just below the lip line as shown in the photo.

- Use the tip of the needle as a digging tool to go under the fabric just below the nose and lift some stuffing toward the surface. All of the following stitches are done inside the face (for this step). Don't pull the thread taut; pull it just enough to create some lift to the upper lip.

- Following illustration (**Q**), anchor a new thread in the back of the head and bring the needle out in the front at the point marked A in the illustration.

- Re-enter at marking A and exit at marking C.

- Re-enter at marking C and exit at marking A. This anchors the thread in the front of the head.

- Re-enter at marking A and exit at marking B.

- Re-enter at marking B and exit at marking A, pulling slight tension.

- Re-enter at marking A and exit at marking C.

- Re-enter at marking C and exit at marking D.

- Re-enter at marking D and exit at marking C, pulling slight tension.

- Anchor the tension by re-entering at marking C and exiting at marking A, and then re-enter at marking A and exit at marking C.

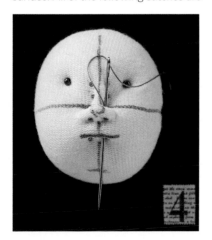

- Run the thread to the back of the head and anchor off. Start a new thread for the next step.

Lower Lip Sculpting, Photo Guide 5

- Bring the new thread from the back of head out at marking A. Anchor the thread by entering at marking C, and then bring the thread back to marking A.

- Re-enter at marking A and exit at marking B.

- Draw seven or eight dots in a large lazy U shape, just below the point where you want the lower lip to end, with the fade-away marker.

- Use the tip of the needle as a digging tool to pierce and lift the stuffing toward the surface of the lower lip area to plump it up.

- Refer to the illustration. Keep all the threads beneath the fabric in a radiating curve shape. Work the thread from the center lip line to the lower lip dots, down and up and down and up, pulling the thread taut as you stitch to create the lower lip. Anchor off the thread in the back of the head behind one of the eyes. Change the thread again if you need to.

- Draw the upper lip in a lazy M shape with wings, as shown, with a brown 005 or 01 tip Pigma pen (**R**).

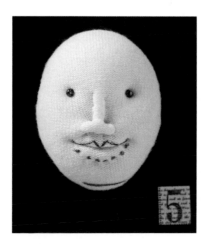

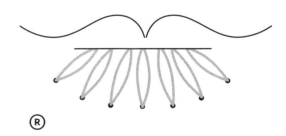

Finishing Lips Sculpting, Photo Guide 5

• Anchor a new thread behind the left eye on the back of the head. Bring the needle through the head at a 45-degree angle and exit at the left corner of the mouth, at the outside edge of the lazy *M* wing. Pull the thread tension slightly to create a smile as you re-enter the thread at the same spot and return the thread to the back of the head and anchor off.

• Travel the thread across the back of the head and anchor it behind the second eye.

• Repeat the first step for the right side of the mouth.

• Ink in the lower lip just at, but not below, the dotted stitch line with the brown Pigma pen.

• Redefine the upper lip, if necessary, with a brown Pigma pen (**S**).

• Draw a line across the face, a generous ¾" (1.9 cm) below the center line of the mouth, with the fade-away marker to indicate the bottom edge of the chin. Measure with the hem gauge for greater accuracy.

Narrowing the Chin Sculpting, Photo Guide 6

• Pierce the knit fabric with the tip of your needle (this is not a stitch) and tug down to create a narrowed chin and jaw. Manipulate the stuffing and move it with your needle to form the shape of a chin.

• Turn the head to the back and stitch as shown in the photograph in a side-to-side overcast stitch pattern. Start from just behind the chin/jaw and stitch halfway up the back of the head. This will narrow the chin and jaw.

• Anchor the thread in the back of the head. Use the tip of the needle to manipulate the stuffing in the chin area, tugging and plumping the stuffing to form a smooth and even chin and jawline.

Tip

If your overcast stitch is too wide, the doll will have a pointed chin but lack a jawline. If this happens, simply cut the stitches, remove them, and try again.

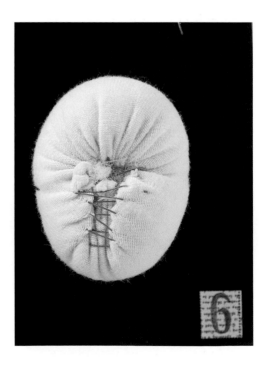

Preparing the Eye Sculpting, Photo Guide 7

• Position the hem gauge across the eye area, from bead to bead, to act as a straight-line guide. Mark a dot on each side of each bead with the fade-away marker.

• Connect the dots in a football shape with the black Pigma pen (005 or 01 tip) to create the outline for each eye. Do not make the lines too big.

• Color the triangle areas on both sides of the eye beads with the white gel pen.

• Anchor a new thread in the back of the head, behind one eye, and bring it out at the outside edge of the football. Re-enter and go directly to the back, pull slight tension and anchor your thread.

• Repeat the last step for the inside corner of the same eye. Travel the thread across the back of the head and anchor it behind the second eye. Bring the thread out at the outside corner of the second eye. Repeat the previous steps for the second eye. Anchor the thread in the back of the head.

• If the eye beads begin to droop after you stitch the corners of the eyes, re-stitch them more tightly to the fabric.

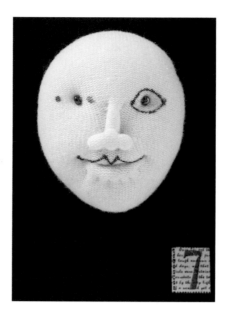

A Final Look at the Soft Sculpting, Photo Guide 8

• It is often necessary to redefine the nostril holes because during stitching the nostril holes may move too far apart. If this happens, mark new nostril dots, closer together, with the fade-away marker. Restitch the nostril holes.

• To define and enhance the cheeks, use the tip of the needle as a tool to lift and pull some stuffing to plump the cheek area. Manipulate the stuffing so the cheeks are high, which keeps the doll young-looking.

TIP

If the thread tension, and therefore the sculpting, appears uneven, restitch the area so it is even and balanced. You can do this any-where and at any time. Be mindful of where the tension is anchored and what you are stitching through.

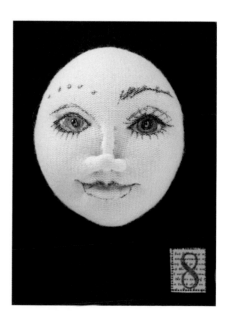

Coloring the Eyes and Face, Photo Guide 9

You will almost always find one side of the face easier to ink than the other. It is helpful to ink your hard side first and then match that work when you ink in your easier side. If you do your best work on your easy side, you will have a hard time balancing the features and keeping the face even.

- To create the iris, draw a circle within the football shape. Color in the iris with a green or blue pastel gel pen or colored pencil. Outline the iris with a green, blue, or brown Pigma pen to define the shape and edge of the iris.

- The black bead is the eye pupil. Redefine and enlarge the pupil with the black Pigma pen, drawing a close circle around the bead. Redefine the top eye line to make it heavier with the same black Pigma pen. Draw the upper eye crease line above the top eye line with the brown Pigma pen.

- Highlight each eye with a small dot of white gel pen in the upper right area (about two o'clock). If the gel pen appears too translucent, use white acrylic paint; dab it on with the tip of your needle.

- Add the lashes as shown with the black Pigma pen. Start drawing each lash at the eye line and stroke outward, slightly beyond the eye crease line (**T**).

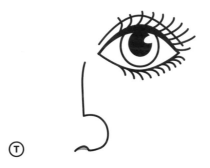

- Draw a dot with the fade-away marker in the arch of each brow. The fade away dots let you check placement before you ink them in. Once you are happy with the placement, ink in the brows in small, short strokes with the brown or black Pigma pens, or a combination of both pens.

- Color in the lips with two different colored pencils; use the darker shade on the top lip and the lighter one on the bottom.

- Redefine the line that divides the top lip from the bottom lip with the brown Pigma pen. It is the lazy *M* shape (page 92). Highlight one side of the lower lip with the white gel pen. If the brown outline seems too dark or harsh, go over it with the white gel pen to soften the outline.

- Apply two colors of blush on the cheeks in a circular motion with an eye shadow sponge applicator. Apply a peach color near the side of the nose (but not on the nostril flares) and a brighter pink on the apple of the cheeks. Dab a bit of blush onto the tip of the nose.

- Define the nostril holes with a sharp, dark gray colored pencil. Add a very shallow *U* shape under each nostril flare. Use the same pencil to draw a short line under the nose to just above the top lip.

- Apply three colors of eye shadow above the eye with a short liner brush. Apply the darkest color in the eye crease line and the other two colors above the eye to just below the brow. Lightly apply color from the brow down and along the side of the nose bridge to highlight.

- Take the head outside and spray the face with a fixative to hold the color. Let it dry completely.

Attaching the Head

Apply clear fabric glue onto the neck stem and glue the head in place (**U**).

Attaching the Hair

I used Tibetan fur as hair on Danielle. You can choose to use loose mohair, mohair yarn, or any other fiber.

To use Tibetan fur cut a strip of skin/hair approximately 2" × 4" (5.1 × 10.2 cm). Tacky-glue the strip in half lengthwise, wrong sides together. Apply the tacky glue to the doll head just along the hairline from above eye level all along the nape of the neck in a big U shape behind the head. Attach the edge of the skin/hair strip over the glue. You need not cover the back of the head because it will be covered with a stunning hat; the hair would add unnecessary bulk (**V**).

(U)

(V)

> ### Tip
>
> Create your own doll hair with mohair yarn. Loosely knit a pot-holder-size square of hair-colored mohair yarn on medium-size knitting needles. Dampen the knitted yarn and place it in a low oven (150°F [65°C]) for about 1 hour or until it is dry. Let the yarn cool thoroughly and then pull the end string to undo the knitting. You will have the most wonderful curly mohair to use for your doll's hair!

Making Danielle's Costume

Making the Pantalets and Knee Scallops

1. Fold the pantalets fabric in half, right sides together, and place the fold line on the pantalets pattern on the fold of the fabric. Trace the pattern twice. Cut along all the lines except the fold line.

2. Open flat the two pieces of fabric and pin them, right sides together, at the crotch seams; stitch (**W**). Then, pin the inseams together, aligning the crotch seams, and stitch (**X**).

3. Turn the pantalets right side out and hand-sew a running stitch with heavy nylon thread ½" (1.3 cm) from the top waist edge, leaving long tails of thread and no knots. Repeat ½" (1.3 cm) up from the bottom of each pant leg (**Y**).

4. Slide the pantalets onto the doll and pull the waist threads tight to gather the pantalets snug. Finger-press the raw edges to the inside. Knot the threads in the back. Dab the knot with tacky glue and bury the thread tails in the torso.

Ⓦ

Ⓧ

Ⓨ

⑤ Pull the leg threads to gather the lower leg openings, just above the knees. Finger-press the raw edges to the inside. Knot the threads tightly so the pantalets fit snugly around each leg. Bury the thread tails.

⑥ Put the two fabrics for the knee scallops right sides together, and trace the scallop pattern twice with a pencil or fade-away marker.

⑦ Stitch the pieces together, taking two stitches straight across the V of each scallop, just as you did when you stitched the hands (page 79). Leave a small opening as indicated on the pattern.

⑧ Cut out the knee scallops with a generous ¼" (6 mm) seam allowance all the way around. Clip into each scallop. Turn the knee scallops right side out, using the hemostats to help. Finger press the seam allowances of the openings to the inside.

⑨ Finger-press (do not use an iron) to smooth and even the scallops. Hand-sew a running stitch along the top edge of each scallop with heavy nylon upholstery thread (**Z**).

⑩ Wrap a scallop around each knee to form a ruffle. Pull the threads to gather it. Knot off the threads in the back and bury the thread tails in the legs. Embellish with ribbons at each knee, as desired.

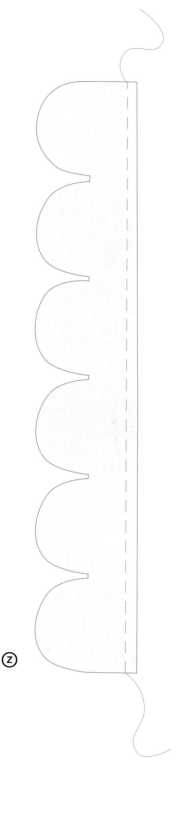

Ⓩ

Making the Upper Arm Puff Sleeve

1. Cut two pieces of silk, each 3" × 8" (7.6 × 20.3 cm). Fold each piece in half, right sides together, and stitch the short edges of each piece together with a ¼" (6 mm) seam to form two circles of fabric. Turn the pieces right side out.

2. Hand-sew a running stitch with heavy nylon upholstery thread along the top and bottom edges of each sleeve puff, leaving long thread tails and no knots. Finger-press the raw edges to the inside.

3. Pull the sleeve puffs onto the doll's arms, up to the shoulders. Pull the top threads to gather the sleeves tightly around the arm and knot off. Bury the thread tails.

4. Pull the thread tails at the bottom edge of the sleeves so they are snug around the arms. Knot off the thread securely and bury the thread tails. The puff sleeve should fit just above the sleeve cuffs that are already on the doll's arms.

5. Glue narrow trim just below the puff sleeve, as desired.

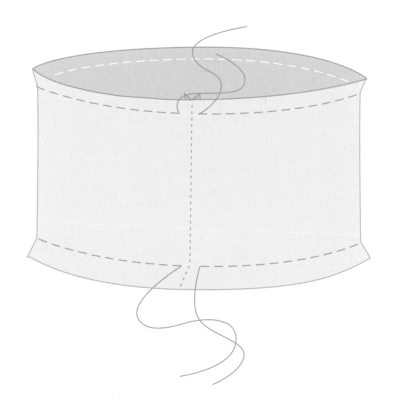

Making and Attaching the Flounces

I used a lovely piece of silk organza that already had a ruffled and pleated edging along one side for the flounces. However, you can choose among many wonderful alternatives, such as narrow gathered lace or strips of tulle, pleated ribbon, or any number of trims. Even rickrack would make a fancy edging and add detail and texture to the skirt flounces.

① Cut two pieces of sheer organza to 6" × 35–40" (15.2 × 88.9–101.6 cm).

② Finish the lower edge and sides of each piece with trim or a narrow hem. Hand-sew a running stitch with heavy nylon upholstery thread across the top edge and side so the threads meet in the middle as shown.

③ Pull the threads to gather the top and sides of each flounce and tie the flounces around the doll's waist, one on each side. Knot off the threads and bury the tails.

④ Trim the loose threads along the waist edge with sharp, small scissors. Glue narrow trim over the waist edge of the flounces to form a waistband and to cover the raw edges.

⑤ Glue silk flowers, velvet leaves, or other embellishments on the center of the waistband, as desired.

> ### TIP
>
> I cut small lengths of trim in three colors and gathered one side to form rosettes for her waist.

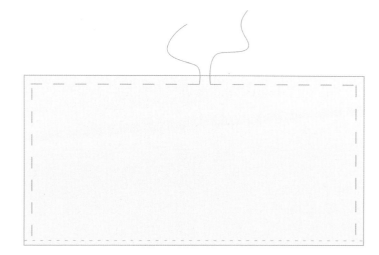

Making the Hat

The hair must be on the doll (page 95) before you start the hat; otherwise, the hat might be too small. The thickness of the hair determines the correct hat size.

① Fold the chosen hat fabric, preferably silk dupioni, in half, right sides together, and trace the hat brim pattern on it twice.

② Stitch directly on the traced line, leaving an opening as indicated on the pattern. Cut out the pieces with a generous ¼" (6 mm) seam allowance. Turn the hat brims right side out.

③ Finger-press and whipstitch the openings closed. Place one hat brim on the front and one on the back of the doll's head, overlapping to fit snugly. Take them off, and tack them securely together. Sew buttons, small flowers, or beads at each side to cover the stitching.

④ Cut a rectangle of the same fabric to approximately 2½" × 6 ¾" (6.4 × 15.9 cm) for the crown of the hat. Fold it in half, right sides together, and stitch a center seam as shown. Hand-sew a running stitch ½" (1.3 cm) from the top raw edge with heavy nylon upholstery thread, leaving long tails

⑤ Pull the threads to gather the crown, tucking the raw ends to the inside as you go. Knot off the thread securely and bury the thread tails. Turn the crown right side out. Finger-press a small hem at the bottom edge to the wrong side.

⑥ Position the crown inside the hat brim, pleating it to fit. Hand-sew the crown and brim securely together. Embellish the front as desired.

⑦ Pull the hat onto the doll's head and pin it securely in place. I don't recommend sewing the hat to the head because the stitching could easily distort the shape of the hat.

Making the Shoes

The upper shoes are made of lightweight leather, suede, or Ultrasuede. You can paint Ultrasuede with acrylic paints or Lumiere paints, which have an iridescent glow. Some leathers and suede can also be painted, but practice on a scrap first. Make the soles from a stiff tooling leather or leather cut from an old belt or leather purse. Cut the leather and suede with very sharp scissors for a smooth edge. Smooth the cut edges of the sole leather with an emery board as needed.

The pattern pieces provided for the shoes are one size; however, the shoes fit differently depending on the stretch of the leg fabric and the shoe fabric. Leather does stretch slightly. Once the shoes are made, try them on the doll. If the shoes are too small, snip off the end of each foot and whipstitch them closed. If the shoes are too big, stuff small bits of fiberfill into the

toes until they fit snugly. If the leather is very soft, the doll's toes might distort the toes of the shoes; in this case, push small bits of stuffing down into the toes of the shoes with the feet already in them. This will help hold the proper shape of the shoes across the toe area.

① Trace two shoe uppers onto the wrong side of one color leather and cut them out directly on the traced line.

② Trace two shoe sling straps onto a different color leather and cut them out directly on the traced line.

③ Trace two soles onto card stock and cut just inside the traced lines. These are referred to as the inner soles.

④ Trace two soles onto the wrong side of the sole leather and cut them out just outside the traced line, so the line remains visible after the soles are cut out. These are referred to as the outer soles. You can use an emery board to smooth the cut edges of the sole leather, if needed.

⑤ Place the inner soles on top of the outer soles. The inner soles should be slightly smaller than the outer; trim the inner soles if necessary.

⑥ Assemble the shoes onto the inner soles. Apply glue along the straight bottom edge of the sling strap on the wrong side of the leather. Wrap the sling strap around the heel of the inner sole, turning the bottom edge under ⅛" (3 mm) to the bottom of the inner sole. Ease the fullness of the heel; do not overlap the edges or clip the excess.

⑦ Apply glue along the toe and outer edges of the upper shoe on the wrong side of the leather. Wrap the piece along the toe edge of the inner sole so it overlaps the sling strap at the sides. Turn the raw edge ⅛" (3 mm) to the wrong side along the bottom of the inner sole. Notice how the two pieces overlap on the sides.

⑧ Once the upper shoe is securely glued in place, poke or punch a hole on each side for shoelaces. A screw-punch makes a clean hole and goes easily through multiple layers of leather.

⑨ Position the outer (leather) soles on the bottom of the shoes and check that they are the correct size; trim them if necessary. Glue an outer sole onto the bottom of each shoe.

⑩ Cut two lengths of ribbon approximately 12" (30.5 cm) long and string them through the punched holes.

⑪ Apply glue to the inside of each shoe, along the edge of the card stock. Slip the shoes on the doll so the centers of the ribbon laces are under the doll's feet. Cross the laces over the ankles and tie them in bows in the front of each leg.

⑫ Trace two shoe toppers on the wrong side of another (or the same) color leather and cut them out directly on the traced lines. If you have a leather hole punch, punch small, decorative holes in the toppers. If you don't have a hole punch, create the same look by dotting each hole on the right side of the leather with a black Pigma pen. If desired, edge the shoe toppers with a gold leaf pen (Krylon's Gold Leafing pen is a good choice).

⑬ Glue the shoe toppers onto the tops of the shoes and embellish them as desired.

TIP

As you glue the shoes together, make sure you center the back sling onto the heel of the inner sole. Then apply the toe piece, making sure it is even on each side and centered at the toe tip, or the shoes will warp and won't fit properly.

Making the Staff

Check your local craft store for unpainted wooden dowels and finials. Paint the finial gold or any other preferred color. Wrap the dowel with ribbons of many colors and glue them in place. Glue the finial and tie short ribbons onto the top of the dowel.

Gallery

Emmaline
by Judy Brown

The biggest challenge for me was the costuming, so I decided to start with the face. I knew if I was happy with the face, the rest of the doll would fall into place, and it did. I sculpted five heads and then chose the one I felt was prettiest.

I chose black silk dupioni with a bright raspberry embroidered floral I had been saving for a special doll. I have a little MacKenzie-Childs bowl with a floral, black and white check, and polka-dot motif that was the inspiration for the coordinating fabrics. I constructed my doll's body and arms of raspberry silk dupioni and her legs of black and white polka-dot cotton. I absolutely adored her body after I jointed her arms and legs, so much that I almost hated to cover her with clothes. I started with a gathered skirt and adorned it with black Venice lace at the hem and a tie at the waist. I made the sleeves with black and white checked silk dupioni, and I made her shoes of black and raspberry leather with a black and white check bow at the toe. I styled her hair from Tibetan lamb and tied it back with a silk ribbon. I am very pleased with how my Emmaline turned out.

Mlle. Pâte à Choux
by Colleen Ehle Patell

Rendered like a French puff pastry, Mlle Pâte à Choux is a veritable work of art. She starts with a solid foundation and has multiple layers of silk, puffed and draped to form a confection of magical delight. I searched my stash for the most gorgeous pieces of silk and auditioned them by laying out several pieces in varied combinations. I finally settled on my color palette of dark burgundy/red, orange, gold, and burnt umber, after looking at the fresh apricots, Bing cherries, and clementines I was assembling for a fruit tart. I was aware that this doll could become a French tart, but I strove to keep her more ladylike and was inspired by thoughts of rich caramel sauce over ripe plums and succulent raspberries topped with crème fraîche.

It might take time to add more layers, but it is not more difficult. I adore collecting beautiful trims and ribbons, and this doll was the perfect excuse to haul them out and use as many of them as I wanted. Her excessive array of silks (I used over fourteen different pieces) may seem extravagant, but it balances the accoutrements of her remaining ensemble perfectly. To make her truly mine, I kept the playfulness that is my usual style and added fringe to her pantaloons, placed art tubes in her hands, and had her hold a swatch of silk and needle felting fusion with beads.

Gigi
by Joan Stephens

Nothing for Gigi was purchased or copied. She already lived in my stash, waiting to be put together and featured. Even the concept of this doll resided within me.

And so, with "pretty and vintage" as my inspirational words, Gigi came to be. Her design just seemed to happen as I became fixated on a gorgeous piece of dupioni that screamed, "Choose me, me, me!" I was so certain that this fabric, with its luscious color and sensuous texture, needed to be used that it became the starting point that brought my doll to life. Yards and yards of shimmering French wired silk ribbon fashioned her skirt and sleeves. Lovely hues of blues and purple batik became her legs and part of her torso. Bits and pieces of antique lace remnants (that might have been a part of a human costume, loved enough not to be destroyed) complemented her outfit. Her ankle-strap shoes were lightly embellished with beads and ornamental trim. The magenta organdy ribbon flower was arranged on top of an old crocheted window blind pull. The blind pull became the crown of her sassy hat. Her hair is a coif of Tibetan lamb.

Anna
by Sally Lampi

Barbara's dolls are always beautiful, young, slim, and full of frills. My dolls, on the other hand, are older and fuller, with lots of spirit and not too much fluff. Some would say they are just fat old ladies having a good time.

I was given the Danielle pattern, with her slim body, long lean legs, and beautiful slim arms. How was I to blend my style with Barbara's pattern? I sewed the torso as provided and then sewed an additional torso from knit fabric and pulled it over the first torso. This provided a second layer that could be manipulated and stuffed. I filled out her tummy, buttocks, and breasts to an ample roundness with fiberfill. I sewed the bodice from a stretch fabric to add even more roundness. Now, this is my vision of a real body.

I used lovely silks in keeping with the pretty style demanded by this Anna doll! Satin shoes on her toes and vintage trims adorn her skirt, making her a vision indeed. I used cotton knit for the face instead of the cotton Lycra blend Barbara uses. This let me drag the cheeks and jowls down to give her a more aged look. I topped her with a head of white hair and voilà! A mature, well-rounded woman ready to step out on the town.

Lady Annabel
by Karen Shifton

Creating Lady Annabel turned into the perfect opportunity to bring out my precious snippets and scraps I had hoarded and saved for a special project. The caramel-colored sari fabric surfaced first and became the main focus of the costume. The embroidered edging was the right scale, and the color enhanced the skin tone of the doll. It also conjured pictures of Englishwomen of the late eighteenth century living in the Far East.

Then, I needed to find examples and pictures from that period. With pictures for inspiration, I searched for appropriate embellishments. Antique laces, tiny braids, silk flowers, and a miniature purse were added to the assemblage.

By the time I finished gathering, I had a full box of possibilities. The fun was in arranging all the potential components and using them to create this wonderful doll.

Miranda
by Marge Thompson

Once I had needle sculpted the head and face, I used Pigma pens and Prismacolor colored pencils, along with just a touch of white and red acrylic paint, to define her features. As soon as I put on the last white dot to highlight her eyes, she immediately told me her name was Mariah and would only be happy dressed in silks!

I found in my stash a wonderful hand-dyed silk chiffon piece that went beautifully with the moss velvet bodice and the yellow georgette sleeves. I used a yellow habotai scarf for her bloomers. I utilized the hand-rolled hem edge as the bottom edge of the bloomers, and the challenge was complete.

Once the body was complete, the clothing created, the head attached, and the shoes constructed, I realized, much to my dismay, that I had used the rib knit side of the knit fabric as the right side for her face. Oh my!

So back to the studio I went to create a second head. Luckily for me, this doll face also wanted a silk outfit, but it was demanding a different name. Miranda, she pleaded, as she also let me know she needed a garnet necklace and silk ribbons in her hair.

Patterns

Chapter 2 – Gabriella's Patterns

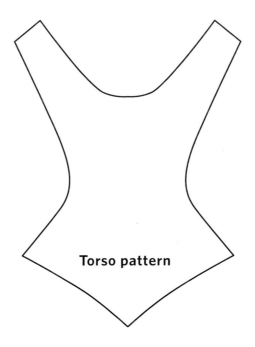

Torso pattern

Flat doll double image

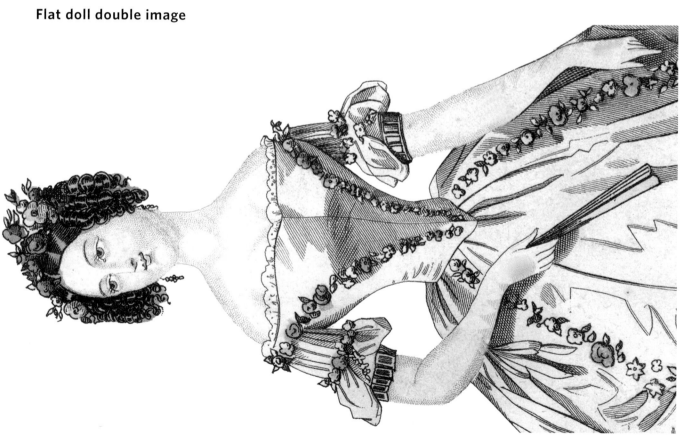

Chapter 3 – Jolie's Patterns

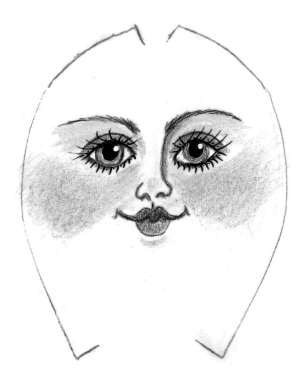

Color photo face transfer

Note: Tape upper and lower pattern pieces together aligning the marking at the knee.

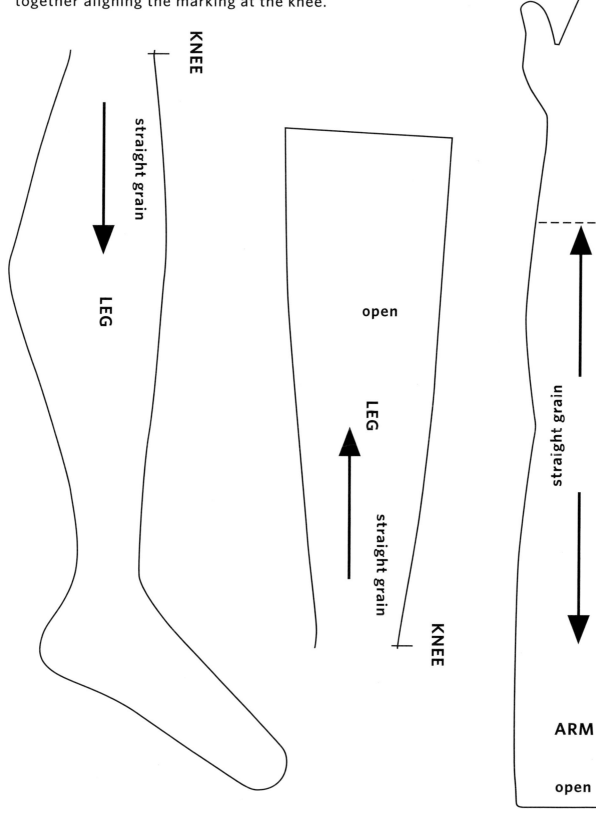

KNEE

straight grain

LEG

open

LEG

straight grain

KNEE

straight grain

ARM

open

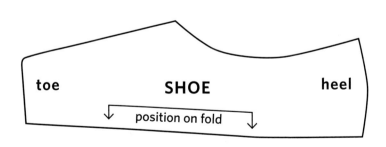

Shoe, Cut-on fold, Toe, Heel

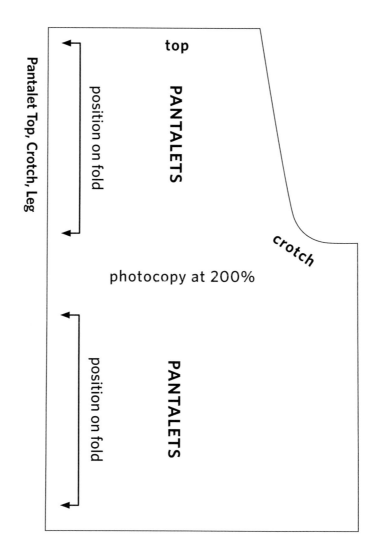

top

PANTALETS

position on fold

Pantalet Top, Crotch, Leg

crotch

photocopy at 200%

position on fold

PANTALETS

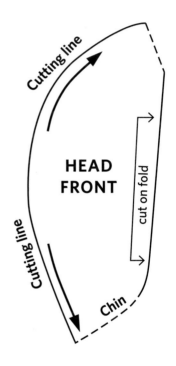

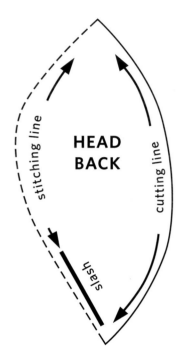

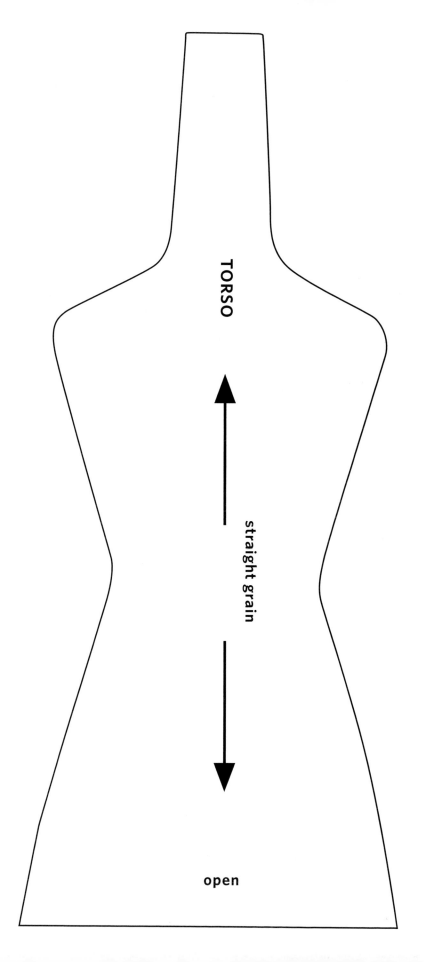

TORSO

straight grain

open

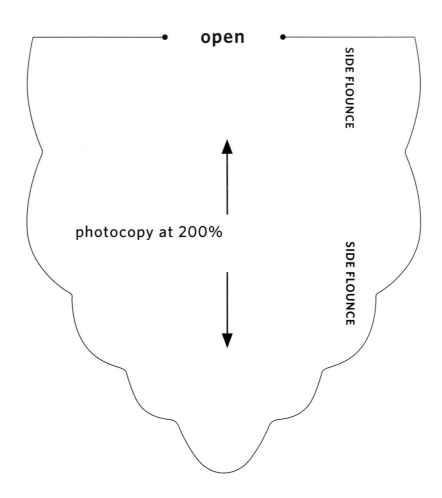

open

SIDE FLOUNCE

SIDE FLOUNCE

photocopy at 200%

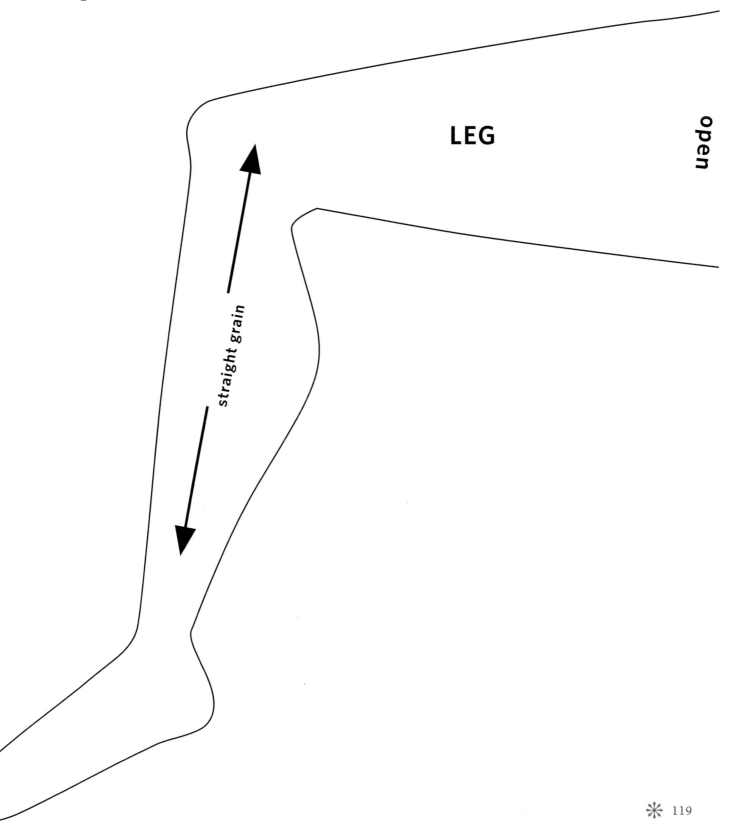

LEG

open

straight grain

SHOE TOPPER

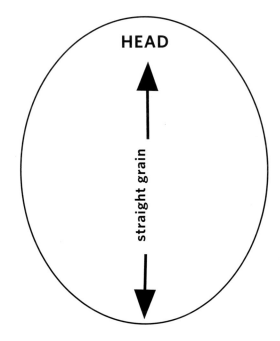

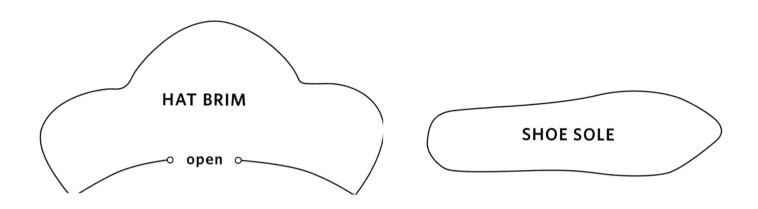

HAT BRIM

open

SHOE SOLE

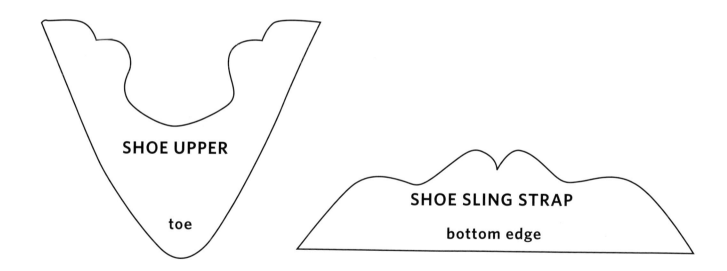

SHOE UPPER

toe

SHOE SLING STRAP

bottom edge

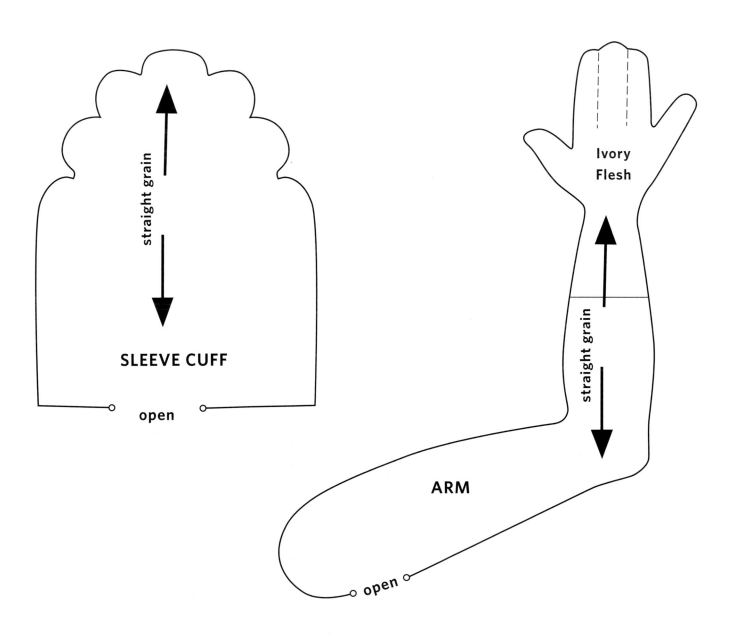

straight grain

SLEEVE CUFF

open

Ivory
Flesh

straight grain

ARM

open

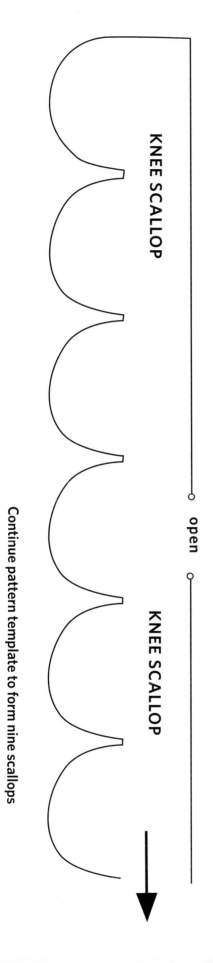

KNEE SCALLOP

open

KNEE SCALLOP

Continue pattern template to form nine scallops

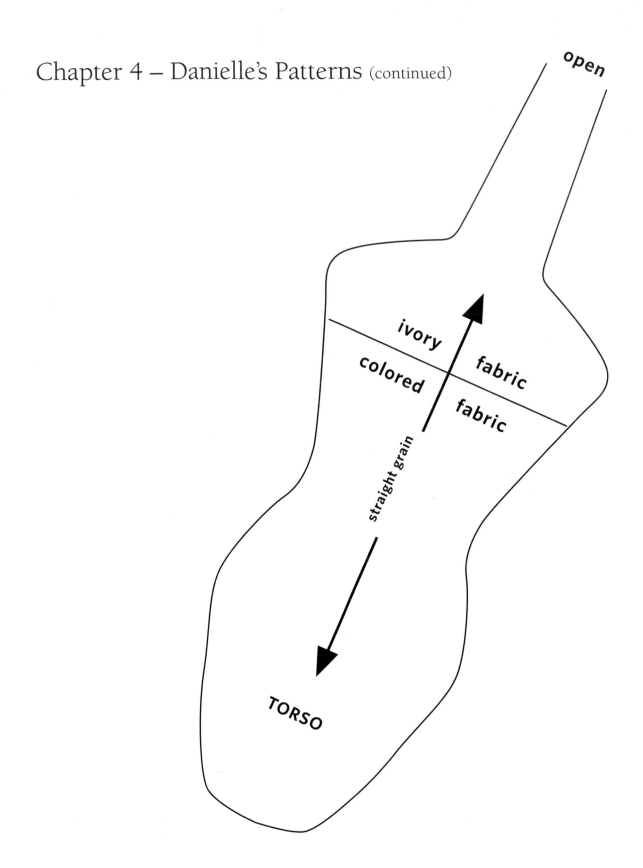

open

ivory

colored

fabric

fabric

straight grain

TORSO

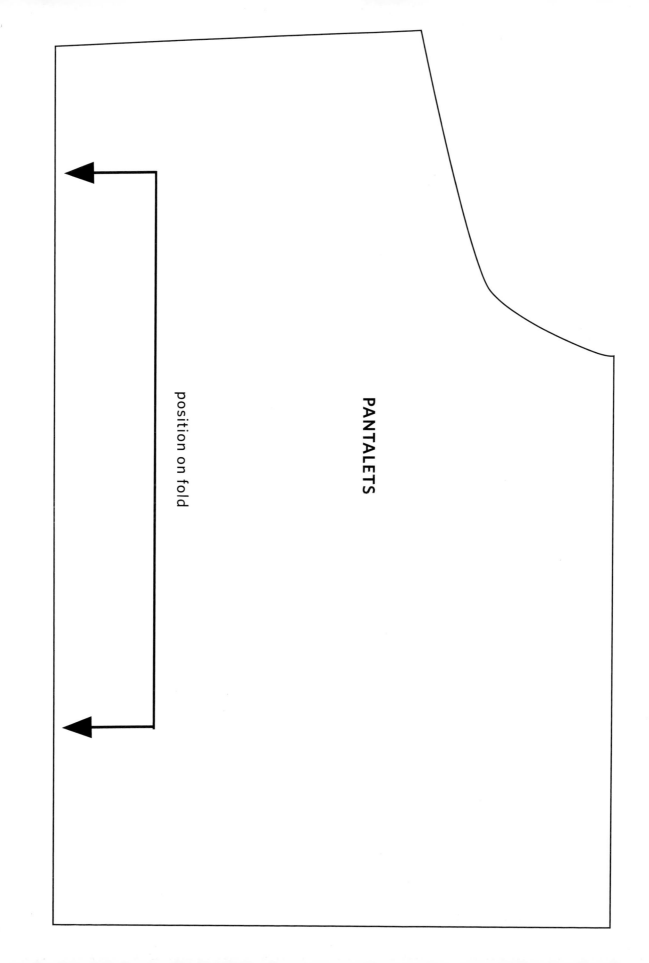

PANTALETS

position on fold

Resources

United States

Barbara Willis Designs

415 Palo Alto Avenue
Mountain View, CA 94041
bewdolls2@aol.com
www.barbarawillisdesigns.com
*Original cloth doll designs, stuffing
forks, pima cotton body fabric,
Tibetan hair fibers*

Elinor Peace Bailey

2001 SE 132 Circle
Vancouver, WA 98683
elinor@epbdolls.com
*Turn-it-all tools, original
designs, fabrics, stuffing forks,
and classes*

Dollmakers' Journey

P.O. Box 523192
Springfield, VA 22152
info@dollmakersjourney.com
www.dollmakersjourney.com
*Cloth doll supplies, fabrics, and
stuffing forks*

Exotic Silks

252 State Street
Los Altos, CA 94022
650.948.8611
www.exoticsilks.com
Large variety of silk, wholesale

M and J Trimming

1008 Sixth Avenue
New York, NY 10018
www.mjtrim.com
*Ribbons, trims, buttons,
beads, crystals*

PMC Designs

9019 Stargaze Avenue
San Diego, CA 92129
jculea@san.rr.com
www.pmcdesigns.com
*Original cloth doll designs, classes,
finger turning tool sets*

Robert Kaufman

129 West 132nd Street
Los Angeles, CA 90061
310.538.3482
info@robertkaufman.com
www.robertkaufman.com
Call for nearest representative
*Fine pima cottons for doll bodies
and costumes*

Rupert Gibbon and Spider

P.O. Box 425
Healdsburg, CA 95448
707.433.9577
service@jacquardproducts.com
www.jacquardproducts.com
*Ink-jet fabric sheets, fiber dyes,
pigment ink pads*

Australia

Anne's Glory Box

60 Beaumont Street
Hamilton, NSW
Australia
*Silk ribbon, cloth doll patterns,
hand-dyed laces, fabrics, and classes*

United Kingdom

Jan Horrox Cloth Doll Supplies

27 Vicarage Road
Cromer
Norfolk, NR27 9DQ
UK
info@jan-horrox.com
www.jan-horrox.com
*Full line of patterns, cloth doll
supplies, and tools*

Rainbow Silks

85 High Street
Great Missenden, Bucks
HP16 OAL
UK
rainbowsilks.co.uk
*Dyes, fibers, trims, silks,
classes, tools*

Contributors

Online Resources

www.clothdollconnection.com
Source for cloth doll events, free patterns, suppliers, designers, online classes, club directory

Fairfield Processing Corporation
www.poly-fil.com/wheretobuy-asp
800.243.0989
Soft Touch Supreme fiberfill

fabricaddictions.com
Online only source for tools, workshops, books, and stuffing forks

clothdollcreations.co.uk
Online only source for stuffing forks, fabrics, patterns, and classes

thingsilike.net
Online only source for patterns, workshops, stuffing forks, and fabrics

joggles.com
Online only source for classes, fabrics, stuffing forks, turning tools and needles

Pamela Armas
GypsyTreasures@cs.com

Colleen Babcock
colleenbabcock@uwclub.net
themagicbean.typepad.com

Elinor Peace Bailey
elinor@epbdolls.com
www.epbdolls.com

Arley Berryhill
arleyberryhill@aol.com
www.arleyberryhill.com

Judy Brown
brownth@aol.com

Patti Medaris Culea
pmcdesigns.com
jculea@san.rr.com

Christine Mary Howard
christinehoward@bigpond.com

Sally Lampi
slampi142@aol.com

Teresa Malyon
teresamalyon@aol.com
www.flights-of-fantasy.me.uk

Sharon Martin
lethashar@aol.com

Jill McCloy
jillmccloy@gmail.com
www.jillmccloydesigns.com

Gloria McKinnon
annesglorybox@bigpond.com.au
www.annesglorybox.com

Ulla Milbrath
ulla@earthlink.net
www.ulla.typepad.com

Colleen Ehle Patell
colleen.patell@gmail.com
wildwackywomendesigns.com

Karen Shifton
kshifton@comcast.net
www.clothingmagic.com

Donna Perry
donna.perry.050@sbcglobal.net

Joan Stephens
dogsngolf@aol.com

Marge Thompson
mmzthompson@yahoo.com

Betts Vidal
bettsbetz@aol.com

Val Zeitler
valzeitler@hotmail.com
www.valsragpatch.com

About the Author

Barbara Willis is a self-taught artist whose main interest lies in fiber figures, the creative process, and ultimately, the presentation. Fibers, color, style, and design elements are her primary focus. Sharing the process with others is the cherry on the whipped cream.

Dolls have been in her life for as long as she can remember, in one form or another. Her journey has been filled with twists, turns, and many round-trips. Sheer persistence and confidence have kept her on track with her doll making and business for over 25 years. Fear of failure was a great motivator once she made the decision to turn her passion into a business. Her passion for her dolls has remained, and the fear of failure has transformed into a feeling of opportunity; opportunities that keep her interested, challenged, and always open to learning.

She shares and teaches doll making in many parts of the United States, Australia, New Zealand, Canada, and England, which has enriched her life and broadened her creative experience and process. Barbara's work has been widely published in magazines, and her dolls have been included in special exhibits, galleries, and books. She resides in the San Francisco Bay Area.

Acknowledgments

My appreciation is widespread to many who have touched my life and rattled my creative spirit.

To my parents Doris and Harry, who let me play in the dirt, build forts, dress my dolls in scraps of fabric, and grow up with a big imagination and lots of love.

To my children Brenna and Jamie. who let me be a kid all over again with them. They taught me so much about what is really important in life.

To my sister, who is my constant helper and always keeps me on track.

To my creative and artistic circle of friends who touch my life daily in some form or other to keep me stimulated, excited, creative, and motivated to take new steps.

A special thank you to the contributing artists for their lovely dolls for the book, as I could not have done this alone. Your dolls are stunning and will be treasured by all who hold this book in their hands. Each one was done with your special style to make the patterns come alive. Bravo and thank you!

To Quarry Books for giving me the opportunity to do this book. Special kudos to Mary Ann Hall for keeping me on track, calm, and confident. You are the magic wand.

Thank you all for your blessings!